WITHDRAWN FROM
SANDWELL LIBRARIES

D0409813

STARS OF THE

'60s

AND WHERE ARE THEY NOW?

STARS OF THE
'60s

AND WHERE ARE THEY NOW?

DEAN HAYES

SANDWELL LIBRARY & INFORMATION SERVICE	
I1772502	
Cypher	05.12.02
796.334092	£14.99

Sutton Publishing Limited
Phoenix Mill · Thrupp · Stroud
Gloucestershire · GL5 2BU

First published 2002

Copyright © Dean P. Hayes, 2002

All pictures courtesy of the *Lancashire Evening Post*.

Title page photograph: Jimmy Greaves, 1968.

British Library Cataloguing in Publication Data
A catalogue record for this book is available from the British Library.

ISBN 0-7509-3001-2

Typeset in 10.5/13.5 Photina.
Typesetting and origination by
Sutton Publishing Limited.
Printed and bound in England by
J.H. Haynes & Co. Ltd, Sparkford.

As the decade opens Tom Finney of Preston North End plays one of his last games in the local derby against Blackburn Rovers at a packed Ewood Park. Here the 'Preston Plumber' tries to go round Rovers' keeper Harry Leyland.

Contents

Bobby Moore and his England team mates after their victory in the 1966 World Cup final.

Introduction

Football was booming in the 1960s with England's World Cup triumph just one of the many highlights in a great decade for English football. For the first time our clubs were winning in Europe: Manchester United became the first English team to win the Champions Cup, ten years after the Munich disaster. And interest in domestic football was still huge. The game was attracting big crowds and football welcomed the 'swinging sixties' as much as any industry.

Tottenham Hotspur earned their place in the history books in the first season of the new decade when they became the first team in the twentieth century to complete the League Championship and FA Cup 'double'. Ipswich Town followed Spurs as champions in 1961/62, winning their only League title under the management of Alf Ramsey, who would have much to celebrate with England four years later. But then the big north-west clubs took centre stage once again, with Everton, Liverpool, Manchester City and Manchester United sharing the next six League Championships before Leeds United snatched the final one of the decade. Liverpool and Manchester United were the only sides to claim the Championship twice and both had great teams. The Anfield club won the title in 1963/64 and 1965/66 with United triumphing in 1964/65 and 1966/67. As always it is impossible to compare teams from different eras but these two would doubtless be right up there among the best of all time. Liverpool had players of the calibre of Ian Callaghan, Roger Hunt and Ian St John while United boasted arguably the best trio of all time with George Best, Bobby Charlton and Denis Law. Interestingly, both sides at the time were managed by Scotsmen: Liverpool by Bill Shankly and Manchester United by Matt Busby.

Profiles of all of the above are included in the hundred top players and ten top managers, which I hope will give you a flavour of how great the 1960s were for English football.

Dean P. Hayes
Pembrokeshire, May 2002

The Players

JOHN ANGUS

Full-back
Born 2.9.38, Amble

LEAGUE RECORD

	A	G
Burnley	438 (1)	4

HONOURS
League Championship 1959/60
1 England Cap

JOHN ANGUS spent his entire senior career at Burnley – a career that spanned three decades. Playing his early football for Amble Boys' Club, he soon caught the eye of one of the shrewdest scouts in the north-east, Charlie Ferguson, who brought him to Turf Moor as an amateur in 1954. At first Angus was homesick and returned home but he was soon back in the fold and the following year, on his seventeenth birthday, signed professional forms. Within a week of his Central League debut, he was unexpectedly drafted into the first team at right-back, after a number of key defenders suffered injuries. Although he had to contend with David Smith for a time to become Harold

Rudman's successor, John Angus was always going to emerge as the long-term choice for the no. 2 shirt.

Angus played his part in Burnley's finest achievement for nearly forty years: the League Championship triumph in 1959/60. He missed just one game during that momentous campaign and his outstanding performances led to him winning a full international cap against Austria in Vienna. It proved to be his only appearance at this level, albeit playing out of position at left-back, though England manager Walter Winterbottom described it as one of the finest debuts he had seen.

Angus took part in a season of near-misses in 1961/62 and continued to impress for the Clarets as the 1960s unfolded and the Championship team began to break up. Remarkably, the attacking full-back hadn't scored a single goal in his League career until a First Division game against Arsenal at Highbury in October 1964. In the days before substitutes were allowed, he was moved up front after suffering an injury and scored both Burnley's goals in a 3–2 defeat!

Towards the end of the 1960s Angus was no longer an automatic choice, though as the decade turned he had forced his way back into the team and was still the man in possession. Following Burnley's relegation in 1970/71, Angus decided it was time to hang up his boots and returned to live and work in his native Northumberland. He made a complete break from football and nowadays spends most of his time improving his already excellent golf game.

LEAGUE RECORD

	A	G
Blackpool	568	6

HONOURS
43 England Caps

JIMMY ARMFIELD
Full-back
Born 21.9.35, Denton

JIMMY ARMFIELD is acknowledged as one of the game's first overlapping full-backs. There is no doubt that his early days as a winger gave him a taste for the attacking aspects of his game. He used to push forwards and when he saw an opening he could cross to good effect, the timing of his runs being perfect.

In his early days at Blackpool in an 'A' team game, he scored two goals from his position on the wing. When the Seasiders' full-back was injured Armfield took his place and was kept in that position. He made his League debut for Blackpool in a 3–0 defeat at Portsmouth on 27 December 1954 and held his place for the next game on New Year's Day, when the Seasiders lost 4–1 at home to Manchester United. An injury to Eddie Shimwell subsequently gave Armfield a chance to establish himself in the first team midway through the 1955/56 season.

> **FACT**
> Blackpool had the unusual experience of achieving more points away than at home in the 1966/67 season. They won only one match at Bloomfield Road (6–0 against Newcastle United) and drew another five. Away they had five wins and four draws, but finished bottom of Division One and were relegated.

After playing for the Football League XI and England Under-23s in a 3–0 win in Italy, Armfield and Jimmy Greaves were flown straight out to Rio de Janeiro. His full England debut in 1959 was in front of 175,000 volatile South Americans. At left-back, he was up against the flying Julinho as England lost 2–0 to the World Cup holders. Perhaps his best international appearance came against Spain at Wembley in 1960. England won 4–2 and Armfield's complete domination of Real Madrid's flying winger Gento earned him a standing ovation.

Jimmy Armfield was a very cultured right-back, sharp in the tackle and quick to recover if his winger went past him. Following his display in the 1962 World Cup in Chile, this brilliant and stylish player was voted the best right-back in the world. He captained England on fifteen occasions after taking over from the injured Johnny Haynes at the start of the 1962/63 season. In fact, at one stage he played in thirty-seven consecutive matches, ending with a total of forty-three appearances.

He helped the Seasiders win promotion to the First Division in 1969/70 but at the end of the following season, after nineteen years with the Bloomfield Road club, Armfield, who had appeared in 627 games, went into management with

Bolton Wanderers. In 1972/73 he led Bolton to the Third Division Championship but in September 1974 he left to manage Leeds United. He took the Yorkshire club to the 1975 European Cup Final but left Elland Road in 1978.

Armfield now works as a journalist and can be heard commentating on a number of radio football broadcasts. He always played with great enthusiasm and was a model player both on and off the field.

LEAGUE RECORD

	A	G
Charlton Athletic	151	20
Wolves	360 (1)	19
Hereford United	13 (3)	1

HONOURS
League Cup 1973/74
2 England Caps

MIKE BAILEY
Wing-Half
Born 27.2.42, Wisbech

MIKE BAILEY, a midfield dynamo who was strong in the tackle and a driving force in attack, was the ideal captain at both Charlton Athletic and Wolverhampton Wanderers where he inspired the other players with his example.

Bailey began his career with non-League Gorleston, playing for the first team when only fifteen years old. Gorleston manager Joe Jobling, a former Charlton wing-half, recommended him to The Valley and he turned professional in March 1959, some eight months after arriving at the club. Bailey made his League debut for the London side the following Christmas and over the next few seasons his performances led to him winning five England Under-23 caps and two more at full international level. The latter were against the United States, a game which England won 10–0 in May 1964, and against Wales later that year.

> In 1965 Wolverhampton Wanderers considered taking the BBC to court over the fictional series 'United', which in the club's eyes was too close a parallel to their own troubled recent history!
>
> **FACT**

In October 1964 Bailey broke a leg in a match against Middlesbrough but recovered well to play in a total of 169 games for the Addicks before being transferred to Wolverhampton Wanderers for £40,000 in March 1966. He made his Wolves debut in a 1–1 home draw against Southampton and appeared in the final eleven games of the season. He helped Wolves win promotion to the First Division in 1966/67 and that season he was voted 'Midland Footballer of the Year'. When Wolves reached the final of the 1972 UEFA Cup against Spurs, Bailey was on the bench, but he skippered the side to victory against Manchester City in the League Cup Final of 1974. Bailey went on to appear in 436 games in all competitions for Wolves, but left Molineux in the summer of 1977 to become player-coach of Minnesota Kicks in the NASL.

Within eighteen months, though, he was back in the Football League with Hereford United, where he got his first taste of management and remained playing until his appointment as manager of Charlton Athletic in March 1980. At The Valley he was appointed too late to prevent the team's relegation to Division Three but they bounced straight back again, promoted in third place. Bailey later managed First Division Brighton and Hove Albion but after steering the Seagulls to a mid-table placing he parted company with the club. He later managed Fisher Athletic and was reserve team coach at Portsmouth before taking over the reins at non-League Leatherhead.

ALAN BALL
Midfielder
Born 12.5.1945, Farnworth, Bolton

HONOURS
League Championship 1969/70
72 England Caps

ALAN BALL was football mad as a boy and went for trials with Wolves and Bolton but was rejected by both. In the end it was only the persistence of his footballing father, Alan Ball senior, that persuaded Blackpool to sign him, after Ball junior had gone to Bloomfield Road and offered to play in a trial.

Within twelve months of making his debut against Liverpool at Anfield in 1962, Ball had become a regular in the Blackpool side. When he first joined the Seasiders, Stanley Matthews – then aged forty-six – had the young midfielder removed from a practice match because, instead of passing to Matthews' feet, he was hitting passes for Stanley to run on to!

After making his England debut against Yugoslavia in 1965, Ball went on to star the following year in the World Cup Finals. Without a doubt his best match was the final itself. His tirelessness, especially during extra time, has become legendary and he set up the third and decisive goal for Geoff Hurst. The sight of him running with his socks down round his ankles during the World Cup Final endeared him to the British public. Around the time of the World Cup Ball thought his career and game were standing still and was ambitious for a move. When it became clear he was

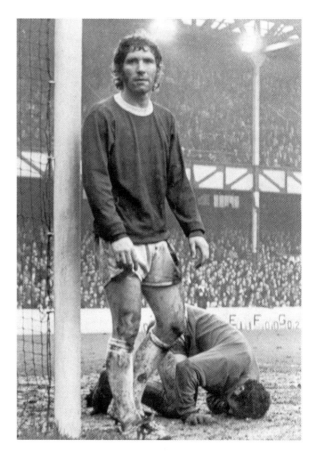

available, there was a lot of interest, especially from Leeds United and Spurs and even from Italian club sides. But in the end Everton moved quickest and on 15 August 1966 manager Harry Catterick signed him for £110,000.

Ball made his Everton debut at Fulham on the opening day of the 1966/67 season, scoring the game's only goal. He was the club's leading scorer in his first two seasons with the Blues and in 1967/68 he scored 20 League goals, 4 of them in a 6–2 win at West Bromwich Albion. Playing alongside Colin Harvey and Howard Kendall in the Everton midfield, he was instrumental in the club winning the League Championship in 1969/70. Ball continued to shine for both club and country, being England's best player in the 1970 World Cup Finals when they tried to defend their title.

FACT

In March 1967 65,000 people watched the Everton v Liverpool derby at Goodison Park and a further 40,000 watched the game on closed circuit television in Stanley Road.

Always a firm favourite at Everton, Ball joined Arsenal in December 1971 for a record £220,000, manager Harry Catterick reasoning that he had gone stale trying to rally a flagging Everton side. After a successful career at Highbury, he moved to Southampton where he made over two hundred first team appearances in two spells. History proves that the departure of Ball signalled the end of a great Everton team. On his 67th international appearance for England, the then manager Don Revie made him captain but five games later he was dropped after breaking a curfew. When he left The Dell, he had a short spell in Hong Kong, later resuming his playing career with Bristol Rovers.

On entering management, Ball took Portsmouth into the First Division before having spells in charge of Stoke City, Exeter City, Southampton and Manchester City, eventually returning to Fratton Park to take charge of Pompey again. Nowadays, Alan Ball is one of a growing band of popular after-dinner speakers.

LEAGUE RECORD

	A	G
Chesterfield	23	0
Leicester City	293	0
Stoke City	194	0

HONOURS
League Cup 1971/72
73 England Caps

GORDON BANKS
Goalkeeper
Born 30.12.37, Sheffield

GORDON BANKS is arguably the greatest goalkeeper of all time. His great save in the 1970 World Cup in Mexico is repeatedly shown on television and is claimed to be the best ever. The save was, of course, from a header from the legendary Pele, who reportedly shouted out 'goal' as soon as he headed it – only to witness Banks throw himself to his right and turn the ball over the bar!

Banks was first noticed in Chesterfield's unexpected progress to the FA Youth Cup Final in 1956 and was still a raw youngster when Leicester City manager Matt Gillies signed him after just twenty-three games for the Spireites. At Filbert Street he developed into one of the best keepers in the country, winning the first of his seventy-three caps for England when he played against Scotland at Wembley in April 1963. The rise of Peter Shilton brought a controversially premature end to Banks' Leicester City career and in April 1967 he joined Stoke City for a fee of £52,000.

> **FACT**
>
> The FA Cup draw for the 1961/62 season matched Chesterfield with Doncaster Rovers and then Oldham Athletic in the first two rounds for the second year running. It was calculated that the odds against this happening were 3,081 to 1.

Banks was the one man who made goalkeeping glamorous but there was nothing pretentious about him. He was outstanding at his job and accepted praise with quiet dignity. Even after England's 1966 World Cup Final success he remained quite unmoved by fame. The Banks Legend took root at Wembley in 1966 and his success and amiable personality lent a new aura and status to goalkeeping. Banks was so influential in England's emergence as a world power in football that coaches and managers began to realise that if they wanted to build successful teams one of their priorities was to find a top quality goalkeeper.

At club level Banks inspired Stoke to their first-ever trophy: the League Cup in 1972 as the Potters beat Chelsea 2–1. He also earned himself the accolade of 1972 'Footballer of the Year'. Why 1972? Did the football writers have to wait until he was on the winning side in a Wembley final? Perhaps it was because he had never played for a fashionable club. Only one other goalkeeper had ever been 'Footballer of the Year' and that was Manchester City's Bert Trautmann in 1956.

Sadly, Gordon Banks's world was shattered on Sunday 22 October 1972. Returning home from the Victoria Ground after treatment for an injury sustained in training the previous day, he was involved in a serious road accident that was to cost him the sight of his right eye. Television programmes were interrupted to advise the public of his accident and his recovery became a national story. He fought hard to regain his position after a long lay-off but was unable to make it, although he played with great distinction for two seasons with Fort Lauderdale in the NASL. After stints of coaching at Stoke and Port Vale and a spell as manager of Telford United, he returned to Filbert Street in 1986 as chairman of the Foxes' short-lived 'Lifeline' fund-raising operation. Subsequently he became involved in the corporate hospitality business and in April 1995 was the beneficiary of a well-attended testimonial game at Filbert Street, where a suite bears his name. An immensely likeable man, his consistency was legendary and he simply was the best!

COLIN BELL
Midfielder
Born 26.2.46, Hesleden

LEAGUE RECORD

	A	G
Bury	82	25
Manchester City	393 (1)	117

HONOURS
League Championship 1967/68
FA Cup 1968/69
League Cup 1969/70
European Cup Winners' Cup 1969/70
48 England Caps

At Manchester City they called COLIN BELL 'Nijinsky' after the racehorse – and with very good reason, for he was one of the fittest and most athletic players in the Football League. He began his career with Horden Colliery Welfare, where his potential was spotted by Bury. He made his League debut for the Shakers against Manchester City in February 1964, shortly before his eighteenth birthday. The following season he was Bury's leading goalscorer and in March 1966, after scoring twenty-five goals in eighty-two games for the Gigg Lane club, he signed for City for a fee of £45,000.

Bell made his City debut just three days after putting pen to paper, scoring in a 2–1 win at Derby County. It was the season that Manchester City won promotion to the top flight after winning the Second Division Championship. The following season, with City back in the First Division, Bell was ever-present and scored twelve goals, including the first of two career hat-tricks in a 3–1 home win over Stoke City. It was his form this season that led to him being selected for a variety of representative matches. He made his England debut in 1968 but it wasn't until after the 1970 World Cup that he began to establish himself in Sir Alf Ramsey's team. His non-stop running and enduring commitment in the infamous World Cup qualifying tie against Poland at Wembley in 1973 weren't enough to earn England a place in the finals.

Bell had been signed for City by Joe Mercer but in 1972, when Mercer left to become general manager of Coventry City, Malcolm Allison, who had been coach since 1965, took over. Allison said of Colin Bell: 'At first he didn't seem to grasp his own freakish strength. He was the best, most powerful runner in the business.'

For a midfield player whose prodigious running was his prime quality, Bell was also an outstanding finisher and in September 1975 he hit his second hat-trick for City as they beat Scunthorpe United 6–0 in a League Cup tie. Bell became the midfield mastermind of the young City side that won the First Division title, the FA Cup, the European Cup Winners' Cup and the League Cup in a four-year spell in the late 1960s and early 1970s. Doubtless he would have made many more than his forty-eight appearances for England had it not been for a serious knee injury that brought his career to a premature end. He was forced to miss the whole of the 1976/77 season. There was, though, time for one further honour: a Central

League Championship medal in 1977/78 before the injury forced him to retire in August 1979.

For a while Bell ran his own restaurant in Manchester before returning to Maine Road as the club's Youth Development Officer. He still works for Manchester City in the commercial department on match days.

LEAGUE RECORD

	A	G
Manchester United	361	137
Stockport County	3	2
Fulham	42	8
Bournemouth	5	0

HONOURS

League Championship 1964/65 and
1966/67
European Cup 1968
37 Northern Ireland Caps

GEORGE BEST

Forward
Born 22.5.46, Belfast

Millions of words have been written about GEORGE BEST, the unknown player from Belfast who became a soccer superstar. He didn't make the Irish Schoolboy team because he wasn't strong or big enough but Manchester United's Northern Ireland scout Bob Bishop rated him highly and signed him up for the Old Trafford club. However, the fifteen-year-old Best was homesick and he and Eric McMordie, later of Middlesbrough, caught the night ferry back to Belfast. Upon Best's return to Old Trafford he settled down under the fatherly influence of Matt Busby and even worked afternoons for the Manchester Ship Canal Company just in case his football career didn't work out! After just fifteen League appearances for United, Best won the first of his thirty-seven caps when he played for Northern Ireland against Wales at Swansea.

Best initially played wide on the left but soon began to adopt a free attacking role, scoring some of the most stunning goals ever seen at Old Trafford. He won a League Championship medal in 1964/65 and again in 1966/67 but then things started to go wrong and his frustration began to show as he retaliated against hard treatment, earning himself a reputation for indiscipline, while his taste for wine and women began to undermine his consistency on the field.

The peak of Best's career came in 1968 when his team won the European Cup at Wembley, beating Benfica 4–1 after extra time. One of those goals was a superb effort by Best, who rounded goalkeeper Henrique before coolly rolling the ball into an empty net. It was a euphoric night for Manchester United, and for Best it was the pinnacle of achievement in a season that saw him gain the titles of English and European 'Footballer of the Year'.

George Best had great natural ability and was one of the most gifted footballers you could wish to see. He had great speed and awareness, coupled with fantastic dribbling ability. Strong and brave, he was the complete all-round forward. He was, however, becoming increasingly difficult to manage – frequently missing training and occasionally failing to turn up for a match!

Just before 1972 United sacked their manager Frank O'Farrell and issued a statement that George Best would remain on the transfer list and would not be selected for Manchester United again. A letter from George Best himself announcing his retirement crossed with this. He walked out on United several times and played his last game for them on New Year's Day 1974. Four days later he failed to turn up for training yet again and his days at Old Trafford were over.

In November 1975 Best joined Stockport County on loan, his drawing power trebling the Edgeley Park club's home attendance. A spell in the States playing for Los Angeles Aztecs followed before he joined Fulham. He later played for Cork in Ireland before returning to America to play for San Diego Sockers, Fort Lauderdale Strikers and San Jose Earthquakes. In 1980/81 he played Scottish League football for Hibernian, returning two seasons later to play for Motherwell. He also turned out for Glentoran, Bournemouth and several non-League clubs.

After a succession of glamorous girlfriends, a drink problem and several skirmishes with the law, Best served a prison sentence in 1985. A footballing genius, George Best now makes public and media appearances, both at home and abroad.

DANNY BLANCHFLOWER

Wing-Half
Born 10.2.26, Belfast
Died 9.12.93

LEAGUE RECORD

	A	G
Barnsley	68	2
Aston Villa	148	10
Tottenham Hotspur	337	15

HONOURS
League Championship 1960/61
FA Cup 1960/61 and 1961/62
European Cup Winners' Cup 1962/63
56 Northern Ireland Caps

DANNY BLANCHFLOWER is one of the most famous players in Spurs' history, not merely because he captained the club to its greatest-ever triumph of the League and FA Cup 'double' in 1961 but also because he was one of the finest players ever to grace White Hart Lane.

Born in Belfast, he was christened Robert Dennis, but somehow became known as Danny to everyone. As a youth, Blanchflower was an all-round sportsman who played football for his school and the local boys' brigade. He studied at Belfast Technical College and was an apprentice engineer for a while. In 1939 he formed his own club called Bloomfield United and so successful was it that he eventually founded a complete league competition. Scout Sammy Weir of Glentoran spotted Danny playing and signed him on amateur forms. It was wartime by now and Danny volunteered for the RAF. He had won a scholarship to St Andrews University and was not called up until he had completed his studies in 1944.

Having signed professional forms for Glentoran, he made his debut as an inside-forward in February 1947, playing for the Irish League against the Football League. His impressive performances for Glentoran led to him joining Barnsley in April 1949. Six months later he made his international debut against Scotland.

Blanchflower was probably too much of an individualist for Barnsley and he questioned their outdated training methods. This led to a move to Aston Villa and he made his debut there on St Patrick's Day 1951 in a 3–2 win over Burnley. His intellectual approach to the game and his passion for trying new ideas met with the same conservative resistance at Villa Park and in December 1954 he joined Tottenham Hotspur.

Danny succeeded Alf Ramsey as captain at Spurs but it wasn't until Bill Nicholson became manager that there was a meeting of minds. It wasn't long before Spurs were the supreme team in English football and honours came thick and fast. Blanchflower captained the side to the League and Cup 'double' in 1960/61 and also scored from a penalty in the Cup Final victory over Burnley the following year. After the disappointment of their semi-final defeat against Benfica in the European Cup in 1962, Spurs went on to win the European Cup Winners' Cup the following season. Blanchflower was voted 'Footballer of the Year' in both 1958 and 1961. He struck up a formidable and fruitful relationship with Peter Doherty, playing in fifty-six out of sixty-two internationals, including forty-one on the trot. With Blanchflower as captain, Northern Ireland reached the quarter-finals of the 1958 World Cup. His playing career came to an end at Old Trafford in April 1964; dropped by Nicholson at the age of thirty-eight, he decided to retire.

A witty, rational and intelligent man, Danny Blanchflower started a career as a journalist for the *Sunday Express*. He gained a reputation for being outspoken and for openly attacking the football establishment. He also created a stir when he refused to appear on *This Is Your Life*, considering it a great invasion of his privacy. In December 1978 he took charge of Chelsea but resigned after three months. He left the *Sunday Express* in 1988 owing to ill health. In May 1990 he received an honour never open to him in his playing days, when Spurs met a Northern Ireland XI in a benefit match. Danny Blanchflower, one of the game's all-time greats, died in December 1993.

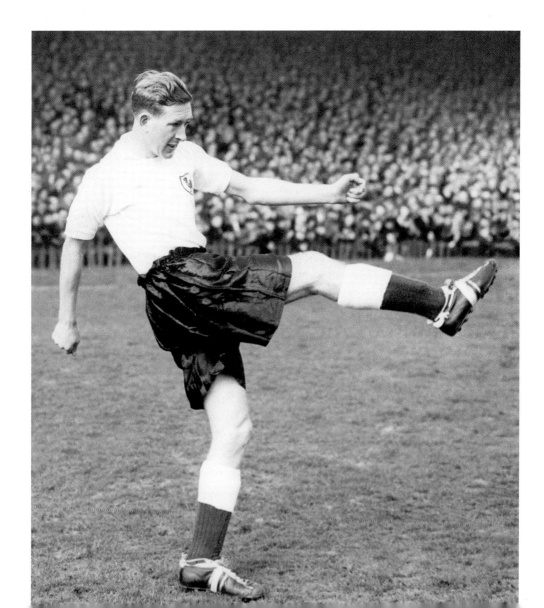

LEAGUE RECORD

	A	G
Stoke City	384 (4)	17
Port Vale	5 (1)	1

HONOURS
League Cup 1971/72

ALAN BLOOR
Defender
Born 16.3.43, Stoke-on-Trent

ALAN BLOOR emerged through the Stoke-on-Trent Schoolboys side to accept apprentice forms at Stoke City and quickly won an England youth international cap, indeed he captained his country at that level. On his seventeenth birthday he became a full professional at the Victoria Ground, but Stoke manager Tony Waddington was determined not to rush him into the first team and he had turned twenty-one before he could claim to be holding down a regular slot in the Potters' League side.

Bloor took over the centre-half berth from Maurice Setters, who had been transferred to Coventry City, and as the 1960s began to unfold he was to play at the heart of the Stoke City defence with Denis Smith. Their partnership was to be the envy of almost every League side in the country. Coveted by many great judges, including Matt Busby at Manchester United, Alan Bloor was the epitome of the resolute defender: calm, undemonstrative, yet a great tackler and a perfect foil to Denis Smith. He also scored some very important goals for the Potters, notably from set pieces.

Alan Bloor completed eighteen seasons at the Victoria Ground. Although medals and caps don't fill his display cabinet, he is the proud holder of a Wembley winners' medal from 1972 when Stoke beat Chelsea 2–1 to win the League Cup and a Watney Cup winners' medal from 1973. He also has the pleasure of knowing that he was an integral member of the most successful side in the history of the club.

In June 1978 Alan Bloor was appointed as the youth team manager at nearby Port Vale. However, he unexpectedly appeared in the Valiants' first team as a substitute at Wimbledon at the start of the 1978/79 season and three days later scored on his full debut in a 5–1 win at Crewe Alexandra. Nevertheless, the following month he reverted to concentrating on his intended management role and was appointed as the club's caretaker-manager in August 1979. A month later he secured the job on a permanent basis but resigned in December 1979 after a string of poor results. Bloor and his assistant Gordon Banks blamed the players' lack of effort for the team's dismal showing.

After football Bloor went into the carpet business in his native Longton before running a newsagent. Now retired, the local lad who made good lives in Trenton.

BILLY BONDS
Midfielder
Born 17.9.46, Woolwich

LEAGUE RECORD

	A	G
Charlton Athletic	95	1
West Ham United	655 (8)	48

HONOURS
FA Cup 1974/75 and 1979/80

BILLY BONDS, an Upton Park legend, was an inspirational leader during his twenty-seven years with West Ham United as a player and a manager. Signed from Charlton Athletic in the summer of 1967, Bonds played in 124 consecutive League matches during his first few seasons with the club before injury ruled him out of the match against Blackpool in October 1970. An England Under-23 international, Bonds was selected for the full international team but had to withdraw through injury and was never given another chance.

In 1974 he succeeded Bobby Moore as captain, leading the Hammers to FA Cup Final victories in 1975 and 1980. He played in the European Cup Winners' Cup Final of 1976 and the League Cup Final of 1981. Having moved into midfield, he ended his first season as captain as the club's leading scorer and netted a hat-trick in a 3–0 home win over Chelsea.

FACT

In November 1960 The Valley, home of Charlton Athletic, witnessed a very strange goal. The home team's winger Lawrie passed the ball back from the half-way line – when keeper Frank Reed was looking the other way! The visitors (Liverpool) won the game.

Having passed Bobby Moore's club record of appearances in 1982/83, Bonds went on to play in 793 League and Cup games for the Hammers, playing his final game at Southampton on 30 April 1988 at the age of forty-one. Earlier that year, his achievements had been recognised by the queen, who honoured him with the MBE. Voted 'Hammer of the Year' on four occasions, he was also presented with the PFA Merit Award in April 1988. When he finally hung up his boots, John Lyall appointed him youth team manager. Although he applied for the manager's job at Upton Park when Lyall was sacked, it went instead to Lou Macari. However, when Macari resigned seven months after arriving from Swindon Town, the ever-popular Bonds was appointed in February 1990. He took the Hammers to one place below the play-off zone in the Second Division that season. In 1990/91, his first full season in charge, he led them to promotion as they finished runners-up to Oldham Athletic. Also in that promotion-winning season, Bonds became the first person in the club's history to be awarded two testimonials. In 1991/92 the club suffered relegation but Bonds' efforts weren't helped by events off the field as fans waged war on the ill-conceived bond scheme. The following season Bonds and assistant Harry Redknapp led the Hammers back into the top flight but after one more season Bonds stunned the Upton Park faithful by resigning. After a spell as Queen's Park Rangers youth team manager, Bonds became manager of Millwall in the summer of 1997 but after just one season at The Den he parted company with the Lions.

One of the greatest names in the history of West Ham United, Billy Bonds now works on radio station XSM.

PETER BONETTI

Goalkeeper
Born 27.9.41, Putney

LEAGUE RECORD

	A	G
Chelsea	600	0

HONOURS
League Cup 1964/65
FA Cup 1969/70
European Cup Winners' Cup
 1970/71
7 England Caps

PETER BONETTI's future in professional football was shaped before he left school – on the day in 1957 when his mother wrote to Ted Drake (then Chelsea's manager) and asked if he would offer a trial to her son who 'might make a useful goalkeeper'. He had that trial in January 1958, joined the Stamford Bridge groundstaff six months later, signed professional forms in April 1959 and made his League debut against Manchester City a year later. From then on he was always first choice. In 1962/63 he helped Chelsea to promotion, in 1964/65 he was in goal when they won the League Cup and in 1967 – the season he was voted Chelsea's first 'Player of the Year' – he made his first appearance at Wembley when Spurs beat them in the FA Cup Final.

Bonetti's daring and spectacular play thrilled the crowds and was a decisive factor in the club's cup triumphs of the early 1970s. In the 1970 FA Cup Final at Wembley he touched world-class in extra time to deny Leeds United the victory their superiority deserved, and in the replay at Old Trafford Bonetti allied bravery to brilliance to bring Chelsea back from the brink of disaster. After being knocked to the ground in a mid-air collision with Mick Jones, Bonetti, his left knee badly swollen, played for the remaining hour of normal time and through the torture of extra time. The injury had left him unable to jump to save the shot from Jones which put Leeds into the lead but the turning point came at 1–1 when twice in a minute he dived to save fierce shots from Terry Cooper. Without such courage the Cup would never have gone to Chelsea for the first time that night.

The following year, in the club's European Cup Winners' Cup triumph in Athens, it was touch and go whether Bonetti would play in the final against Real Madrid because pneumonia had kept him out of the quarter-finals and semi-finals in which John Phillips had proved an admirable deputy. But in Athens, manager Dave Sexton went for experience. After Chelsea had been shocked by Zoco's 89th minute equaliser, Bonetti produced three superb saves and Chelsea lived to fight again two nights later. In the replay Chelsea led 2–0 with just over ten minutes to go but a goal by Fleitas revived the Spanish side and the closing minutes belonged to Bonetti. Twice he was off the line to block shots by Amancio and seconds from time came one of his greatest saves when he sprang to the left and caught Zoco's point-blank header. Despite these two outstanding performances, sandwiched in between was one nightmare game: England, 2–0 up with twenty minutes to play, lost 3–2 to West Germany after extra time and Bonetti bore the brunt of the criticism.

After being given a free transfer he spent a summer playing in American football but returned to Stamford Bridge on a monthly contract, helping Eddie McCreadie's young team win promotion in 1976/77. He continued to battle for a first-team place for two seasons, taking his total of appearances to 728 before moving to the Isle of Mull in 1979, combining life as a guest-house proprietor with occasional appearances for Dundee United. He also worked as a postman before returning to his beloved Chelsea as the club's goalkeeping coach.

Now living in Birmingham, Bonetti, who was recently involved with the England set-up, coaches goalkeepers at a number of League clubs.

TONY BOOK
Full-Back
Born 4 September 1934, Bath

LEAGUE RECORD

	A	G
Plymouth Argyle	81	3
Manchester City	242 (2)	4

HONOURS
League Championship 1967/68
FA Cup 1968/69
League Cup 1969/70
European Cup Winners' Cup
  1969/70

TONY BOOK, a latecomer to full-time football, did not kick his first ball in League soccer until just before his twenty-ninth birthday. It was Malcolm Allison who discovered Book when he was the manager of Southern League Bath City. When Allison moved to Plymouth Argyle, he took Book, who was working as a bricklayer, with him and in two seasons at Home Park Book missed only three games, becoming a great favourite with the Pilgrims' fans.

Allison, now Joe Mercer's assistant at Manchester City, persuaded his boss to sign Book for £17,000 and he made his debut in a 1–1 draw at Southampton in August 1966. He missed only one League game in his first two seasons with City

before his career looked to be over following an Achilles tendon injury late in 1968. However, upon his return to first-team action, City had a great cup run which climaxed when they beat Leicester City 1–0 at Wembley in the 1969 FA Cup Final. At the end of the season Book was voted 'Footballer of the Year' with Derby County's Dave Mackay. He was back at Wembley the following year, carrying off the Football League Cup and seven weeks later the European Cup Winners' Cup as City beat Gornik Zabrze 2–1.

Tony Book retired from playing in 1973 and joined Manchester City's coaching staff. He later became assistant-manager to Ron Saunders and when Saunders left Maine Road in 1974 Book took over as City manager. He soon found some success as a manager when City won the Football League Cup in 1975/76 and were runners-up in the First Division in 1976/77. In the summer of 1979 Book was made general manager with Malcolm Allison returning as team manager, and he later had an important behind-the-scenes role. Working with the younger players he found some outstanding players to create a team that won the FA Youth Cup for the first time in 1986. In November 1989 he was appointed caretaker-manager after Mel Machin was sacked and became first-team coach under Peter Reid in the early 1990s. Today Tony Book still works with Peter Reid, scouting for Premier League Sunderland.

LEAGUE RECORD

	A	G
Leeds United	585 (1)	90
Hull City	61	6
Doncaster Rovers	2 (3)	0

HONOURS
Division Two Championship 1963/64
League Cup 1967/68
League Championship 1968/69 and
  1973/74
FA Cup 1971/72
UEFA Cup 1967/68 and 1970/71
54 Scotland Caps

BILLY BREMNER
Midfielder
Born 9.12.42, Glasgow
Died 7.12.97

BILLY BREMNER, the combative midfield dynamo, was the driving force behind the success story of Leeds United in the 1960s and 1970s. A truly inspirational figure, he gave wonderful service to the club he joined as a seventeen-year-old in December 1959 after being rejected by both Arsenal and Chelsea for being too small. Always determined in the tackle and no mean passer, he made his Leeds debut alongside Don Revie against Chelsea the following month. In his early days at Elland Road he often brushed with football's authorities but gradually matured and collected many honours. Later, as captain, he was the man who ensured that the manager's instructions were carried out on the field. In many ways he epitomised the Leeds spirit of that time. He hated losing and between the club winning the Second Division Championship in 1963/64 and 1975 he rarely finished on the losing side. His collection of honours included two League Championship medals (1968/69 and 1973/74), an FA Cup winners' medal (1972) and two UEFA Cup winners' medals (1967/68 and 1970/71).

Because of Leeds' mean streak and Bremner's own aggression, he was never high on the popularity list among many opposing supporters but everyone in the game recognised the contribution he made to Leeds United's success. He was voted 'Footballer of the Year' in 1970 when Leeds were runners-up in both the League Championship and the FA Cup and in a distinguished international career he won fifty-four Scottish caps. A fiery competitor, Bremner was sent off – along with Kevin Keegan – during the 1974 FA Charity Shield at Wembley. Both players removed their shirts and as a result both were fined £500 and their suspensions meant that each missed eleven matches.

Bremner moved to Hull City in September 1976 and ended his playing career after joining Doncaster Rovers as player-manager in November 1978. He played only a handful of games at Doncaster. Within two years of his appointment he took Rovers to promotion when they finished third behind Southend and Lincoln in Division Four. Bad luck and crippling injuries saw them relegated in 1982/83 but they bounced back the following season as Division Four runners-up.

A year later he was offered the ultimate post as manager of his beloved Leeds United, then in the Second Division. In 1986/87 they reached the FA Cup semi-

finals and the Division Two play-offs, and Bremner's reward was an extended contract. However, they seemed to go backwards the following season and Bremner was axed. He returned to take charge at Doncaster but parted company with the club in 1992. He was then in great demand as an after-dinner speaker, until his death at the age of fifty-four in December 1997.

LEAGUE RECORD

	A	G
Chelsea	174 (2)	80
Birmingham City	83	37
Queen's Park Rangers	72	31
Millwall	77	27
Brighton & Hove Albion	56 (10)	14

HONOURS
League Cup 1964/65
4 England Caps

BARRY BRIDGES
Centre-Forward
Born 29.4.41, Norwich

BARRY BRIDGES made his Football League debut for Chelsea when he was seventeen, scoring in a 3–2 win over West Ham United in February 1959. Yet two years elapsed before he was given another chance to prove himself as the Blues slid towards relegation in 1961/62. During that season Bridges scored nineteen goals in thirty-two games but the following term he failed to maintain that striking rate as Chelsea played Second Division football. He was dropped to accommodate Frank Upton but later returned to resume his prolific partnership with Bobby Tambling. Most of his goals were scored from close range, his speed and outstanding awareness enabling him to strike on a ball played into the six-yard box before anyone else had moved!

Bridges' consistency in front of goal won him full international honours against Scotland, Yugoslavia and Hungary during the 1964/65 season but at the end of that campaign he was one of eight Chelsea players sent home from Blackpool after they had broken a curfew imposed by Tommy Docherty. The following October he was recalled into the England team for the match against Austria but three days after this game he was dropped from the Chelsea starting line-up against Leicester to make room for Peter Osgood.

Bridges was upset that his World Cup chances were now being jeopardised and asked for a transfer but following a

petition by outraged fans who didn't want their hero to leave Stamford Bridge he withdrew his request and moved into a wandering role at the expense of Bert Murray. Though he was very successful in this new role, he was sent home from the airport prior to the first leg of an Inter Cities Fairs Cup tie against Barcelona and it was no surprise when he left Chelsea in May 1966 to join Birmingham City.

Bridges continued to find the net for the St Andrew's side, topping the club's scoring charts in 1967/68 with twenty-nine League and Cup goals. He appeared in the League Cup and FA Cup semi-finals of 1967 and 1968 but in August 1968 he was transferred to Queen's Park Rangers. After injuries had hampered his progress during his first season at Loftus Road, he top-scored in 1969/70, in the process netting both goals in a 2–1 home win over his former club. He later played for Millwall and Brighton and Hove Albion before leaving to play in South Africa in 1974. He later managed Irish clubs St Patrick's Athletic and Sligo Rovers before he returned to Horsford in Norfolk where he took a milk round and managed a couple of the local non-League sides.

GERRY BYRNE
Full-Back
Born 29.8.38, Liverpool

LEAGUE RECORD

	A	G
Liverpool	273 (1)	2

HONOURS
Second Division Championship
  1961/62
League Championship 1963/64 and
  1965/66
FA Cup 1964/65
2 England Caps

When Bill Shankly arrived at Anfield in December 1959, the career of full-back GERRY BYRNE was going nowhere. He had joined the staff in 1955 straight from school and had made just two first team appearances, scoring an own goal on his debut! His performances for the club's Central League side were only moderate and he had been placed on the transfer list at his own request. In fact, Gerry Byrne had the hallmarks of a player who would be on the fringes of big-time football for a number of years before drifting towards a lower grade. However, following an injury to Ronnie Moran, Gerry Byrne stepped in to give a series of accomplished performances and when Moran returned to first-team action Byrne kept his place by switching to right-back in place of Dick White. During the Reds' promotion-winning season of 1961/62, Byrne was ever-present as Liverpool won the Second Division Championship, finishing eight points ahead of runners-up Leyton Orient.

Following the emergence of Chris Lawler, Byrne reverted to left-back to replace the ageing Moran. Over the next seven seasons Byrne proved himself to be one of the most reliable defenders in the First Division. Though he wasn't the quickest of full-backs, he was one of the greatest readers of the game and ferocious in the tackle. His performance in the 4–0 aggregate defeat of Belgian champions Anderlecht in the 1964/65 European Cup competition was described by Bill Shankly as 'the best full-back display Europe has ever seen'.

Gerry Byrne's finest moment came at Wembley in 1965 as the Reds met Leeds United in that season's FA Cup Final. He played for just under two hours with a broken collar bone, overcoming great pain and hiding his discomfort from Don Revie's side. It was Byrne who laid on Liverpool's first goal in extra time. Taking an inch-perfect pass from Willie Stevenson, he reached the by-line before crossing the ball for Roger Hunt to head home. Though he enjoyed success at club level, the Liverpool defender was less successful on the international front. He was capped twice by England at full international level, though in the first of his two outings he was given the run-around by Scotland's Willie Henderson.

At Anfield, Byrne was a member of the Liverpool side that won the League Championship in 1963/64 and 1965/66 but a knee injury sustained in a 3–2 win over Leicester City on the opening day of the 1966/67 season meant that he was never quite the same dominant force again. Sadly recurring knee trouble prompted the popular defender's retirement in 1969 after which he joined the club's coaching staff for a while. Shanks was warm in his praise for one of the surest defenders in the top flight when he said: 'When Gerry went it took a big chunk out of Liverpool. Something special was missing.'

On leaving Anfield Byrne worked as an odd-job man at the Pontins Holiday Camp in Prestatyn, North Wales, but the knee trouble flared up again and he was forced to give up work.

	A	G
Liverpool	637 (3)	50
Swansea City	76	1
Crewe Alexandra	15	0

HONOURS
Second Division Championship
  1961/62
League Championship 1963/64,
  1965/66, 1972/73, 1975/76 and
  1976/77
FA Cup 1964/65 and 1973/74
UEFA Cup 1972/73 and 1975/76
European Cup 1976/77
4 England Caps

IAN CALLAGHAN
Outside Right
Born 10.4.42, Liverpool

IAN CALLAGHAN joined Liverpool straight from school and made his League debut as a teenager in a 4–0 win over Bristol Rovers in April 1960, after just four outings in the club's Central League side. Yet it was another season and a half before he was given a regular spot in the Reds' side as they won promotion to the First Division. In the top flight Callaghan's game blossomed. He was fast and direct, getting to the by-line to feed Hunt and St John with the type of crosses that brought the strikers plenty of goals. He was no great scorer himself but two of his efforts are worth recalling. Against Everton in 1963 his spectacular 30-yarder sank the Blues as Liverpool headed for their first League Championship, while against Inter Milan in the 1965 European Cup semi-final he side-footed home from an acute angle after Stevenson and Hunt had worked a well-rehearsed free-kick routine.

Though on the small side and slightly built, Callaghan was a courageous and determined player. An old-fashioned winger at Liverpool, he was turned into a central midfield player – his appetite for the ball and work-rate being a great influence in the formative years under Bill Shankly. He played only four times for England, scant reward for such an outstanding club career. He played twice under Alf Ramsey in 1966 but it was eleven years before he added to his collection, when manager Ron Greenwood decided to try a block of seven Liverpool players against Switzerland. Callaghan was thirty-five when he played his last international game – and the fact that he was even considered at that age speaks volumes for his fitness and durability.

Ian Callaghan was not a player to grab the headlines but he always gave a fully committed performance for the ninety minutes. He had tremendous standards of dedication, loyalty and skill, embodying the qualities which built Liverpool into probably the greatest club side in the world. He won five League Championship medals, one Second Division Championship medal, two FA Cup winners' medals, two UEFA Cup winners' medals and a European Cup winners' medal. In 1974 he was voted 'Footballer of the Year'. Liverpool's longest-serving player, the last of his 848 appearances for the Reds was on 29 March 1978 in a European Cup semi-final first leg against Borussia Moenchengladbach.

On leaving Liverpool Callaghan went to Swansea, helping his old team-mate John Toshack lift the Swans out of the Third Division. After leaving The Vetch, he had spells with Cork Hibernian and Soudifjord of Norway before ending his career with Crewe Alexandra. Never cautioned by a referee, Ian Callaghan well deserved the MBE awarded to him for his services to football.

Still enjoying the occasional round of golf with former Reds Roger Hunt and Ron Yeats, Ian Callaghan lives in Ormskirk and along with Geoff Strong owns the Hesketh public house in Rufford. He also works part-time for the Littlewoods pools panel.

BOBBY CHARLTON
Forward
Born 11.10.37, Ashington

LEAGUE RECORD

	A	G
Manchester United	604 (2)	199
Preston North End	38	8

HONOURS
League Championship 1956/57,
  1964/65 and 1966/67
FA Cup 1962/63
European Cup 1968
106 England Caps

BOBBY CHARLTON, nephew of the legendary Jackie Milburn, offers a host of memories: sweeping crossfield passes of great majesty, deadly shooting from long range and, above all, great sportsmanship. A product of Manchester United's famous youth team, Charlton was a member of the sides which won the FA Youth Cup in 1954/55 and 1955/56. He made his first-team debut standing in for Tommy Taylor on 6 October 1956, scoring twice in a 4–2 win over Charlton Athletic. On 5 February 1958, after a European Cup tie in Belgrade, the United plane crashed in thick snow at Munich Airport. Bobby Charlton was thrown 50 yards and escaped with just a deep cut on his head. He returned to his native north-east and was about to give up football altogether, but his doctor persuaded him to kick a ball around a local park. Within days, thankfully, he was back at Old Trafford, determined to play in memory of his friends who had died at Munich. It didn't take long for Charlton to reach the footballing heights, for within a little over two months he made his international debut against Scotland, marking the occasion with a spectacular goal.

> In 1967/68 Manchester United had a League attendance average of 57,758: a record in the history of the competition. The following season they sold 1,554,540 copies of their official programme *United Review* – a record for a club programme.
>
> **FACT**

By 1966, and the World Cup Finals in England, Charlton's skills had reached their full maturity. He opened England's account against Mexico with a typical long-distance blast and went on to score some thrilling goals in the tournament, including both the goals in England's 2–1 semi-final win over Portugal. At the end of that season, he won both the 'Footballer of the Year' and European Player awards. In 1967 he won his third League Championship medal, though his finest moment was yet to come. In May 1968 he scored two goals in the emotionally charged European Cup Final against Benfica at Wembley, as United won 4–1. He walked off the pitch in tears, one of the few footballers ever to achieve all their major ambitions.

After 106 caps and 49 goals, his international career ended in Mexico in the 1970 World Cup in dramatic fashion. He was substituted in order to keep him fresh for the semi-finals as England led West Germany 2–0 – but it wasn't to be as the Germans ran out the winners 3–2. In 1973 Bobby Charlton pulled on a Manchester United shirt for the last time at Stamford Bridge. He had set appearance records for both club and country and had become a footballing legend. He joined Preston North End as player-manager but didn't enjoy the same level of success off the field and duly retired from management in 1975.

Bobby Charlton took up a position with a travel company as well as being an active director of Wigan Athletic, which he managed for a brief spell at the end of the 1982/83 season. He established the famous Bobby Charlton soccer schools for children, which have helped so many young players of all ages and abilities to improve their skills. Manchester United honoured him with a place on the board and in 1994, after earlier being awarded the CBE for his services to football, he was knighted. Sir Bobby Charlton, one of the most talented and popular footballers of all time, is still a director of his beloved Manchester United.

LEAGUE RECORD

	A	G
Leeds United	628	70

HONOURS

Second Division Championship 1963/64
League Cup 1967/68
League Championship 1968/69
FA Cup 1971/72
UEFA Cup 1967/68 and 1970/71
35 England Caps

JACK CHARLTON
Centre-Half
Born 8.5.35, Ashington

JACK CHARLTON, known as 'Big Jack', was part of the Elland Road scene for over twenty years. His uncles George, Jim and Jack Milburn all started their careers with Leeds United and it was Jim who recommended the gangling youngster to the Yorkshire club. After National Service with the Royal Horse Guards, Jack began to occupy the centre-half spot vacated by Welsh international John Charles, who had switched to attack. A hard, uncompromising defender, Charlton played for the Football League against the League of Ireland in 1957 and it seemed to be only a matter of time before he won full international honours. However, his career reached a plateau as he found himself in a struggling Leeds United team. He also had a brief spell as captain, but he gave it up because of his superstition about coming out on to the pitch last!

After helping Leeds win the Second Division Championship in 1963/64, Jack Charlton, with Norman Hunter alongside him, began to develop into the best centre-half in England. A supreme header of the ball and an excellent tackler, he won a belated first international cap in 1965 against Scotland, when his brother Bobby, already a household name with Manchester United, was also in the side. The brothers played vital roles in England's 1966 World Cup success and Jack won a total of thirty-five caps, his last against Czechoslovakia in the 1970 World Cup Finals in Mexico. Voted 'Footballer of the Year' in 1970, he won an array of top domestic honours. He won a League Championship medal in 1968/69, an FA Cup winners' medal in 1972, a League Cup winners' medal in 1966/67 and UEFA Cup winners medals in 1967/68 and 1970/71.

A year after winning his FA Cup medal, Charlton left Elland Road to become manager of Middlesbrough. In his first season at Ayresome Park he was named Manager of the Year as Boro swept to the Second Division title by a record points margin. In October 1977 he took over as manager of Sheffield Wednesday and revived their flagging fortunes before leaving for a brief spell as boss of Newcastle United.

In February 1986 he was appointed manager of the Republic of Ireland. The first Englishman to hold the post, he steered them to the European Championship Finals in 1988, where his side pulled off a famous victory over England. To prove that Irish success was no fluke, in 1990 he led the Republic to

the World Cup finals for the first time. They reached the quarter-finals before losing to the hosts Italy. Such deeds earned Jack Charlton the Freedom of Dublin. In January 1996, after the Irish just failed to qualify for that year's European Championships, Jack retired. He is still active on the after-dinner speaking circuit but spends most of his time nowadays pursuing his major interest of fishing.

LEAGUE RECORD

	A	G
Walsall	72	41
Fulham	85 (1)	45
Leicester City	36	12
Leeds United	270 (3)	110
Barnsley	47	15

HONOURS
FA Cup 1971/72
League Championship 1973/74
UEFA Cup 1970/71
19 England Caps

ALLAN CLARKE
Forward
Born 31.7.46, Willenhall

ALLAN CLARKE came from a footballing family – brothers Wayne, Frank, Derek and Kelvin all played League football – but he was the pick of the crop. An instinctive goalscorer, he represented Birmingham Schools and South East Staffordshire Boys before joining Walsall as an apprentice in 1961, turning professional in August 1963. He soon began knocking in goals for the Saddlers and in March 1966 he joined First Division Fulham for £35,000. He made his Cottagers' debut as a substitute for Johnny Haynes in a 3–1 home defeat by Leeds United before making his first full appearance in the return match at Elland Road four days later as Fulham gained revenge with a 1–0 win. In 1966/67 Clarke was Fulham's leading scorer with twenty-nine League and Cup goals, a total which included a hat-trick in a 5–1 home win over Newcastle United. He topped the charts again the following season, scoring four times in a 6–2 League Cup defeat of Workington. Following Fulham's relegation in 1968 Clarke demanded a move and Leicester City paid a club record of £150,000 for his services. He soon ingratiated himself with the Filbert Street faithful, scoring all three goals in a 3–0 win over Manchester City as well as the FA Cup semi-final winner against West Bromwich Albion. Voted 'Man-of-the-Match' in Leicester's 1969 FA Cup Final defeat by Manchester City, he left the Foxes to join Leeds United when the Yorkshire club's manager Don Revie paid a British record fee of £165,000 to take him to Elland Road.

Nicknamed 'Sniffer' in recognition of his clinical penalty-area poaching skills, he played in three FA Cup Finals for the Yorkshire club (scoring the winning goal in 1972), won a League Championship medal in 1973/74 and also scored in their UEFA Cup victory of 1970/71. Clarke, who won nineteen full caps for England, had scored 151 goals in 366 games for Leeds United when he left in June 1978 to become player-manager of Barnsley.

After helping the Oakwell club out of the Fourth Division in his first year of management, his drive and ambitious approach prompted the Leeds board to bring him back to Elland Road at the start of the 1980/81 season. After finishing in mid-table that season, United were relegated in 1981/82 and Clarke found himself out of a job. Scunthorpe United offered Clarke a way back to management but life at the Old Show Ground was a struggle and he rejoined Barnsley before ending his managerial career with a brief spell at Lincoln City.

'Sniffer' now lives in Scunthorpe and is working as a representative for a firm manufacturing ventilating extractors for industry.

Manchester United's Sadler outjumps Allan Clarke.

LEAGUE RECORD

	A	G
Blackburn Rovers	579 (2)	15

HONOURS
35 England Caps

RONNIE CLAYTON
Wing-Half
Born 5.8.34, Preston

RONNIE CLAYTON was only sixteen when he made his Football League debut for Blackburn Rovers in 1950/51. His early promise led the then Rovers' manager Jackie Bestall to predict an England future for the talented youngster. Clayton had natural leadership qualities which showed early in his career. In September 1955 he won his first Under-23 cap and a month later he appeared for the England 'B' team. In November of that year he completed the international sequence making his debut for the full England team.

Clayton was a tremendous driving force in Blackburn's promotion back to the First Division in 1957/58. An energetic wing-half, he was strong in the tackle and a brilliant timer of the ball in the air. He provided the Ewood fans with many magic moments during his long career, but few can rival his vital equalising goal in the FA Cup tie against Liverpool during Rovers' promotion-winning season of 1957/58. A full house at Ewood witnessed this sixth-round tie. With just ten minutes remaining Liverpool led 1–0 when Clayton, Rovers' courageous captain, returned to the field after touchline treatment. He was just in time to line up for a free-kick awarded against the Reds. Roy Vernon lobbed the ball to the far post, where Clayton, moving more quickly than anyone else, flung himself forward to connect with his forehead and send the ball into the roof of the net. It completely changed the course of the game, for a minute later Ally McLeod grabbed the winner. It wasn't until the following Monday that it was discovered that Clayton had in fact chipped his kneecap.

He appeared in the final stages of the 1958 World Cup in Sweden and succeeded Billy Wright as captain for the last five of his thirty-five England appearances. He continued to give good service to Blackburn and led them to the 1960 FA Cup Final, only for them to lose 3–0 to Wolverhampton Wanderers.

Remaining loyal to what many would class as an unfashionable club, Ronnie Clayton experienced the highs and lows but always maintained the same level of enthusiasm and endeavour. At the end of the 1968/69 season he left Ewood Park to become player-manager at Morecambe. He returned to Ewood in December 1970 for a well-deserved testimonial before going back to north-east Lancashire to team up with Great Harwood. On leaving the game, he worked for twelve years as a representative with ATS tyres. Now, as well as playing golf and turning out in charity games, he still attends all home games at Ewood Park.

GEORGE COHEN

Right-Back
Born 22.10.39, Kensington

LEAGUE RECORD

	A	G
Fulham	408	6

HONOURS
37 England Caps

England international full-back GEORGE COHEN made his Fulham debut in a 2–1 home defeat at the hands of Liverpool in March 1957. It was his only appearance that season but midway through the 1957/58 campaign he won a regular spot in the Fulham side, helping the club reach the FA Cup semi-finals where they lost to Manchester United. In 1958/59 he missed just one game as the Cottagers won promotion to the First Division and over the next nine seasons the speedy full-back missed just a handful of games through injury. In 1961/62 he helped the club to another FA Cup semi-final and then, in May 1964, he won the first of thirty-seven full caps for England against Uruguay at Wembley. Cohen was a member of the England side that won the World Cup in 1966, forming a formidable full-back pairing with Ray Wilson. He was the last Fulham player to win an England cap!

The popular defender received a nasty knee injury in a First Division game against Liverpool in December 1967. Though he tried to make a comeback, the

injury virtually ended his career, during which he had scored six goals in 459 League and Cup games. Subsequently he had a brief spell coaching the juniors at Craven Cottage before leaving to develop his business interests. He now combines his interests in building and property development with raising money for cancer charities.

CHARLIE COOKE
Midfielder
Born 14.10.42, St Monance (Fife)

LEAGUE RECORD

	A	G
Chelsea	289 (10)	22
Crystal Palace	42 (2)	0

HONOURS
FA Cup 1969/70
European Cup Winners' Cup 1970/71
16 Scotland Caps

CHARLIE COOKE, a Scottish winger in the traditional mould, had the ability to beat defences on his own. He began his career with Aberdeen before moving to Dundee, where he won full international honours. He joined Chelsea in April 1966 for a club record fee of £72,000, as a direct replacement for Terry Venables. In his early days at Stamford Bridge he found it impossible to adapt to the team's established style. He was moved out to the wing to provide pin-point crosses for Tony Hateley, but he never seemed to produce his best form on the flanks.

Always needing to be at the heart of the action, his ball-juggling skills made him hugely popular with the Stamford Bridge crowd and in 1967/68 he was voted the Blues' 'Player of the Year'. When Dave Sexton took over the reins at Stamford Bridge he wasn't convinced about Charlie Cooke's contribution and the Fife-born player soon realised he would have to harness his individualism to the collective effort of the team. In 1969/70 he seemed a more rounded performer and was still very effective when given the chance in the middle of the park. Few will forget his performance in the FA Cup Final replay at Old Trafford when he outshone Billy Bremner and created Peter Osgood's goal with an exquisite chip.

FACT

Chelsea won an FA Cup fourth-round replay at home against Preston North End in January 1969 by 2–1 despite being a goal down at full time. They scored twice in the two minutes of injury time added on by the referee.

Charlie Cooke was a player who could be relied on to produce his best on the big occasion and in the matches against Real Madrid in Athens he was outstanding. Yet in spite of these performances, he couldn't find the consistency to earn a regular place in the Blues' midfield and in September 1972 he followed Paddy Mulligan to Crystal Palace. He spent fifteen unhappy months at Selhurst Park before returning to Stamford Bridge in the wake of Alan Hudson's departure. He had cost just £17,000, but it was soon clear that the Blues had secured a bargain. Playing wide on the left, his displays were inspired. Sadly, despite having rediscovered his old passion for the game, he began to suffer a series of niggling injuries. Nevertheless he was able to help guide Eddie McCreadie's young team to promotion in 1976/77. Cooke left Stamford Bridge at the end of the following season, and went to the United States where he played for Los Angeles Aztecs, Memphis Rogues and California Surf. He subsequently decided to settle there and now lives in Cincinnati where he runs a very successful soccer school.

LEAGUE RECORD

	A	G
Chester City	94	44
Luton Town	32	21
Norwich City	113	58
Southampton	239 (1)	134
Portsmouth	59	18
Manchester United	0 (8)	0
Millwall	3	0

HONOURS
29 Wales caps

RON DAVIES
Centre-forward
Born 25.5.42, Holywell

RON DAVIES began his football career at Chester City, where he was made to jump hurdles wearing army boots during training, an experience the Welsh international later claimed gave him extra power when jumping for crosses. On leaving Sealand Road he joined Luton Town, where he netted twenty-one goals in thirty-two games, including four against his next club, Norwich City. Davies arrived at Carrow Road in September 1963 for £35,000 – a record fee for both clubs. At Norwich he scored fifty-eight goals in 113 League matches including twenty-six in one season and when he was sold to Southampton for £55,000 in the summer of 1966 there was a public outcry in East Anglia.

Davies, already capped by Wales, ended his first season in the top flight as the First Division's leading scorer with thirty-seven goals in forty-one games. His tally included four in a 6–2 win over Aston Villa and hat-tricks against Leicester City and Burnley. This was a remarkable record in a Southampton side that struggled all season against relegation. In the course of netting

> **FACT**
>
> During a Division Four match at Aldershot on New Year's Day 1966, Chester had the misfortune to lose both full-backs, Ray Jones and Bryn Jones, with broken legs.

those thirty-seven goals he scored in ten successive league games for the club. In 1967/68 he scored twenty-eight goals to make him the First Division's joint top-scorer for the second year in succession, including four in a 6–2 win at Chelsea. He top-scored again the following season with twenty goals in thirty-eight games. In 273 League and Cup games for the Saints, he scored 149 goals overall.

Davies joined Southampton's south coast rivals Portsmouth in the summer of 1973 and appeared in all the club's competitive matches the following season, scoring sixteen goals. The season after that he signed for Manchester United but his powers were waning and he registered only eight substitute appearances without scoring. After a short spell at Millwall he hung up his boots and became a demolition worker for a while. He also proved that he had a great talent with his hands as well as his feet by selling art sketches – including portraits of players he had played with and against.

In 1988 he moved to the United States where he still lives in a luxury house within an acre of secluded woodland outside Orlando. The former Welsh international is still involved with the game, coaching the local semi-professional side, Orlando Lions.

WYN DAVIES
Centre-Forward
Born 20.3.42, Caernarfon

LEAGUE RECORD

	A	G
Wrexham	55	21
Bolton Wanderers	155	66
Newcastle United	181	40
Manchester City	45	8
Manchester United	15 (1)	4
Blackpool	34 (2)	5
Crystal Palace	3	0
Stockport County	28 (2)	7
Crewe Alexandra	50 (5)	13

HONOURS
Inter Cities Fairs Cup 1968/69
34 Wales Caps

In his early career Welsh-speaking WYN DAVIES worked in a Llanberis slate quarry, having been discovered in the Caernarfon and District League by Arthur Lunn, the Caernarfon Town manager. It was while playing with his home-town team in the Welsh League that he was spotted by a Wrexham scout. Davies went on to be a member of the Robins side that enjoyed a lengthy run in the League Cup, and he scored a number of vital goals. In his last match for Wrexham, Davies was one of three players who scored a hat-trick in a 10–1 win over Hartlepool United.

When he moved to Bolton Wanderers, Davies became affectionately known as 'Wyn the Leap' owing to his amazing heading talents in the centre-forward position. Quickly installed into the no. 9 shirt, he was a regular in the Wanderers' side for four-and-a-half years. In 1964 he won the first of thirty-four caps for Wales when he played against England at Wembley. He scored his first hat-trick for the Lancashire club in a 3–0 win over Southampton and ended that 1964/65 season as the Wanderers' top scorer with twenty-five goals. His performances for the Wanderers led to his name being linked with a number of top clubs and in October 1966 he left Burnden Park to join Newcastle United for a club record fee of £80,000.

FACT

During the second half of the FA Cup fourth-round replay between Preston North End and Bolton Wanderers at Deepdale in February 1966, it was discovered that both North End full-backs, Ross and Smith, were wearing no. 3 shirts!

He was the Magpies' first superstar of the modern game, though he was a reluctant hero, being a somewhat reserved character. Though his ball skills never matched his aerial ability, he held the ball up well and controlled the forward line. Very much a provider of chances, the target man up front, he was never lethal in front of goal, though he did grab his share of goals, mostly with powerful headers into the back of the net. As the Magpies surged into European competitions, Davies became one of the most feared strikers on the continent, scoring ten goals in twenty-four games and helping the club win the Inter Cities

Fairs Cup in 1969. However, once the club had been eliminated from Europe the following season, Newcastle manager Joe Harvey decided to dispense with Davies' style of play, and after recovering from an injury he signed for his long-term admirer Joe Mercer at Manchester City. But Davies remained only briefly at Maine Road before moving across Manchester to Old Trafford. Any hope of an Indian summer disappeared with the appointment of Tommy Docherty as manager. After a short spell with Blackpool, Davies headed south for an equally brief stint with Crystal Palace. Stockport County signed him in August 1975 before his long career ended with Crewe Alexandra.

Davies retired from senior football in 1978 but continued playing in the Northern Premier League with Bangor City and also in South Africa's National Football League for the Pretoria club Arcadia Shepherds. He later returned to England and settled in Bolton, working for Warburtons as a baker, though he still holds on to the dream that one day he will have a smallholding in his native Caernarfon.

DEREK DOUGAN
Centre-Forward
Born 20.1.38, Belfast

LEAGUE RECORD

	A	G
Portsmouth	33	9
Blackburn Rovers	59	26
Aston Villa	51	19
Peterborough Utd	77	38
Leicester City	68	35
Wolves	244 (14)	95

HONOURS
League Cup 1973/74
43 Northern Ireland Caps

DEREK DOUGAN was known wherever he played as simply the 'Doog'. He began his career in Ireland with Distillery before signing professional forms for Portsmouth in August 1957. He remained at Fratton Park until March 1959 when he was transferred to Blackburn Rovers for £15,000. A year later he had scored the two semi-final goals that beat Sheffield Wednesday to take Rovers through to the FA Cup Final against one of his future clubs, Wolverhampton Wanderers. He posted a transfer request on the morning of the Cup Final, which ten-men Rovers lost 3–0.

Following Gerry Hitchens' departure to Inter Milan, Aston Villa splashed out £15,000 for the popular Irishman's services. During his time at Villa Park Dougan amused many with his adoption of a shaven head and scared more with his propensity for off-field scrapes, but after two years he was on the move again, this time to Peterborough United. Perhaps this spell in the Third Division helped to restore his sense of perspective, or perhaps a renewed

> Aston Villa had the unusual experience of achieving more points than they scored goals in 1968/69 in Division Two. In their forty-two matches they scored only thirty-seven goals – but obtained thirty-eight points and escaped relegation!
>
> **FACT**

burst of media interest in 'The Doog' when Posh met Arsenal in the FA Cup rekindled his ambitions. At any rate Dougan took a pay cut to join Leicester City back in the top flight. Leading City's forward line with his unique flair, he lapped up the crowd's adulation, not least on the occasion when he netted a flamboyant hat-trick against his former club, Aston Villa. Shortly before the transfer deadline in 1967, Wolves' manager Ronnie Allen moved in and secured Dougan's services for a fee of £50,000.

In just over eight seasons at Molineux Dougan scored 123 goals in 323 League and Cup appearances. He helped the Wanderers clinch promotion from the Second Division in 1966/67 and then collected a League Cup winners' medal in 1974. In between times he played his part in Wolves' UEFA Cup run to the final in 1971/72 and while still an active member of the team became Chairman of the Professional Footballers' Association. Capped forty-three times by Northern

Ireland, Derek Dougan was one of the game's great characters. Forever involved with officialdom, he was sent off at least half-a-dozen times in his colourful career.

A stimulating author and entertaining television pundit, he surprised few when he later moved into management, albeit with Kettering Town. In 1982, seven years after leaving Molineux, he returned to Wolves as chief executive, a position he held only briefly before circumstances forced him out of office. He later became involved in raising money for various charities and worked on several committees, some related to soccer. Dougan now lives in Codsall where he works as a marketing and PR consultant.

LEAGUE RECORD

	A	G
Manchester City	441 (7)	32
Stoke City	115	5
Bolton Wanderers	40	2
Rochdale	24	1

HONOURS
Second Division Championship 1965/66
League Championship 1967/68
FA Cup 1968/69
League Cup 1969/70 and 1975/76
European Cup Winners' Cup 1970/71
5 England Caps

MIKE DOYLE
Central Defender
Born 25.11.46, Manchester

MIKE DOYLE was a very determined player in whatever position he was given. He made his first-team debut for Manchester City as a centre-forward against Cardiff City in March 1965 following a series of impressive displays for the youth and Central League sides. His influence during the 1965/66 season went a long way towards helping City climb out of the Second Division. He was not a prolific goalscorer, but when he did score they were usually important goals. He scored six goals in a four-match spell over the Christmas period that season to help consolidate City's position at the top of the division. Doyle was also instrumental in City topping the First Division in 1967/68. It was during this season that he played his first representative game, playing for England Under-23s against Hungary and for Young England against an England XI. There followed appearances for the Football League, the first in 1972 against the Scottish League.

Doyle seemed to save his goals for the European competitions or for the domestic trophy finals. He scored the equalising goal at Wembley in the 1970 League Cup Final after West Bromwich Albion had gone a goal up, and in April 1970 he scored one of the goals in the European Cup Winners' Cup semi-final second leg against Schalke, City winning 5–1 on aggregate after losing by the only goal in Germany. Doyle also scored against Gornik Zabrze in the 1970/71 European Cup Winners' Cup campaign. His goal made it 2–2 on aggregate and forced a third match in Copenhagen which City won 3–1. Unfortunately City lost to Chelsea in the two-legged semi-final, with Doyle missing both matches through injury.

Mike Doyle was one of Manchester City's finest players under Mercer and Allison and later Tony Book, winning two League Cup winners' medals, an FA Cup winners' medal and a European Cup Winners' Cup medal. After Rodney Marsh left Maine Road in 1975 Doyle was made club captain and a year later made the first of his five full international appearances for England against Wales. After struggling to get back into the City side after injury, he was transferred to Stoke City in the summer of 1978. After playing in over a hundred games for the Potters, he joined Bolton Wanderers, later playing for Rochdale before hanging up his boots.

He worked as a sales manager for Slazenger for over ten years and is now employed in the insurance industry, although he still commentates regularly on local radio.

TONY DUNNE
Full-Back
Born 24.7.41, Dublin

LEAGUE RECORD

	A	G
Manchester United	414	2
Bolton Wanderers	168 (4)	0

HONOURS
FA Cup 1962/63
League Championship 1964/65 and
  1966/67
Second Division Championship
  1977/78
European Cup 1967/68
33 Republic of Ireland Caps

Just a few weeks after winning an FAI Cup winners' medal with Shelbourne in April 1960, TONY DUNNE was on his way to Manchester United. A centre-forward in his junior days in Dublin with St Finbar's and Tara United, he worked his way up through the ranks at Old Trafford, before claiming a regular first-team spot in place of Noel Cantwell halfway through the 1961/62 season. That breakthrough signalled the beginning of his career as one of the greatest full-backs the game has ever seen.

He made his full international debut for the Republic of Ireland in a 3–2 home defeat by Austria in April 1962, going on to appear in thirty-three games, appearing in both full-back and centre-half positions. He also played alongside his brother Pat in the Irish side in the mid-1960s and captained the national side four times.

Tony Dunne had thirteen seasons at Old Trafford during which he turned out for the Reds in 530 League and Cup games. He picked up League Championship medals in 1964/65 and 1966/67 (missing just two games during those seasons), an FA Cup winners' medal after United's 3–1 victory over Leicester City in the 1963 final and a European Cup winners' medal in 1968. It was in that epic European Cup Final, in which United defeated Portuguese champions Benfica 4–1, that the football pundits reckon Dunne gave one of the greatest displays of his career: he frustrated the Benfica attackers with resolute defending, moved forward at every opportunity and curved long accurate passes into the paths of United's front men. His contribution was officially recognised in Ireland when he was voted 'Footballer of the Year' for 1969.

In April 1973 Tony Dunne was one of six players – including Denis Law – to be freed by United boss Tommy Docherty and the following August, over thirteen years after arriving in Manchester, he was transferred to Third Division Bolton Wanderers. In five seasons at Burnden Park Dunne played in 192 League and Cup games and in his final season in the Football League, 1977/78, he won a Second Division Championship medal with the Wanderers. He then jetted off to the United States to play for Detroit Express in the NASL.

Tony, who still follows the fortunes of the Wanderers, now lives in Sale and manages the golf driving range he built in Altrincham shortly after hanging up his boots.

MIKE ENGLAND
Centre-Half
Born 2.12.41, Holywell

LEAGUE RECORD

	A	G
Blackburn Rovers	165	21
Tottenham Hotspur	300	14
Cardiff City	40	1

HONOURS
FA Cup 1966/67
League Cup 1972/73
UEFA Cup 1971/72 and 1973/74
44 Wales Caps

A member of Blackburn Rovers' FA Youth Cup winning side of 1958, MIKE ENGLAND played for the Ewood Park club at outside-right, half-back and centre-forward before settling in central defence where he was acknowledged as arguably the best young centre-half in the country. Though he made his League debut in a 4–1 home defeat at the hands of Preston North End in October 1959, it was 1963/64 before he established himself as the club's first-choice centre-half. He made his debut for Wales against Northern Ireland in April 1962 and by the time of his £95,000 transfer to Tottenham Hotspur in August 1966, England, who had scored twenty-one goals in 184 League and Cup games for Rovers, had won twenty-one full caps to go with his eleven at Under-23 level. The fee was a Football League record sum for a defender.

England was a worthy replacement for Maurice Norman. Lean, strong, quick and brave, he was Spurs' defensive kingpin for the next nine years and hardly missed a game except through injury. He was also sometimes pushed upfield into an emergency centre-forward role where he acquitted himself well. In his first season at White Hart Lane he helped the club lift the FA Cup, giving a superb performance in the final to dominate Chelsea centre-forward Tony Hateley. Although he missed the 1971 League Cup Final with an ankle injury, he helped Spurs win the 1972 UEFA Cup and the 1973 League Cup. He also appeared and scored in the 1974 UEFA Cup Final.

Few forwards were able to get the better of Mike England, whether he was playing for Spurs or Wales. In March 1975, aged thirty-three, troubled by ankle problems and with Spurs struggling against relegation, he quite suddenly announced his retirement but re-emerged the following August to play for one more season with Cardiff City, having spent the summer with Seattle Sounders. He helped Cardiff to promotion from the Third Division and then spent four further American summers playing for Seattle, appearing for Team America in the 1976 Bi-Centennial Tournament with England, Brazil and Italy.

England returned to Britain's shores to take the Welsh manager's job and had seven-and-a-half seasons in charge, during which period Wales were desperately unlucky not to qualify for the final stages of the major tournaments under his straight-talking honest guidance. In 1984 England was awarded the MBE for his services to Welsh soccer. On leaving football, he became a businessman in his native North Wales and now owns residential homes in the holiday resorts of Rhyl and Colwyn Bay.

JIMMY GABRIEL
Wing-Half
Born 16.10.40, Dundee

LEAGUE RECORD

	A	G
Everton	255 (1)	33
Southampton	190 (1)	25
Bournemouth	53	4
Swindon Town	6	0
Brentford	9	0

HONOURS
League Championship 1962/63
FA Cup 1965/66
2 Scotland Caps

JIMMY GABRIEL, a powerhouse of a right-half, became one of the most expensive teenagers in British football when he joined Everton from Dundee for £30,000 in March 1960. Understandably, the young man needed time to settle and in only his third senior outing he was hopelessly outclassed by West Bromwich Albion's England international Derek Kevan, who scored five times as Everton were beaten 6–2 at the Hawthorns. However, Gabriel reacted positively, volunteering for extra training to hone his fitness as he began to acclimatise to the more rigorous demands of the English game.

Gabriel went on to build a fine career for himself. His strong, forceful style, particularly effective in defence, made him the near-perfect foil for the more adventurous wanderings of Brian Harris on the opposite flank. However, there were times when he contributed several stirring performances as an emergency centre-forward, scoring from this position in the 3–1 victory over Liverpool in February 1964. When Brian Harris lost his place to Tony Kay midway through the 1962/63 season, Gabriel continued to complement his midfield partner, helping the Blues win the League Championship. He was also a leading light in the club's 1966 FA Cup Final victory over Sheffield Wednesday.

> The latest time at which any first-class football match finished was 10.10pm at The Dell on 5 December 1960. In a League Cup match between Southampton and Leeds United a power failure caused a 62-minute hold-up.
>
> **FACT**

Despite such success, Gabriel was not destined to see out his prime with the Goodison club. Only twenty-six years old, Gabriel was sold to Southampton the following summer, where he contributed five years' sterling service. He was just the sort of player the Saints needed at that time and when he left to play for Bournemouth in July 1972 he was sorely missed. After just over a year with the Dean Court club, he moved to North America where he played for Seattle Sounders.

In the summer of 1990 Gabriel returned to Goodison Park to help Blues' manager Colin Harvey look after the first team, later taking over as caretaker boss at either end of Howard Kendall's second reign. Despite all the managerial changes at Everton, Jimmy Gabriel remained part of the coaching set-up and exerted a particularly valuable influence on the Blues' youngsters until he left Goodison in the summer of 1997 and headed for the United States. However, it is as an accomplished top-flight performer when the Blues had their backs to the wall that Everton fans will forever remember Jimmy Gabriel.

Jimmy Gabriel is fourth from left in the dark shirt.

JOHNNY GILES
Midfielder
Born 6.11.40, Dublin

LEAGUE RECORD

	A	G
Manchester United	99	10
Leeds United	380 (3)	88
West Bromwich A	74 (1)	3

HONOURS
FA Cup 1962/63 and 1971/72
League Cup 1967/68
League Championship 1968/69 and
   1973/74
UEFA Cup 1967/68 and 1970/71
59 Republic of Ireland Caps

JOHNNY GILES was a product of the famous Dublin football nursery, Home Farm. He left Dublin at the age of fifteen to join Manchester United. He rose through the ranks at Old Trafford and graduated to the first team in September 1959. He won an FA Cup winners' medal in 1963 after United's 3–1 victory over Leicester City but was then surprisingly sold to arch rivals Leeds United for £32,000. In fact, it has been said on many occasions that the worst decision the Old Trafford club ever made was to let Giles join the Yorkshire side.

A brilliant tactician with one of the game's shrewdest brains, the former winger was transformed by Leeds' manager Don Revie into one of the greatest midfield dynamos of the 1960s and even the 1970s. In his first season at Elland Road he helped Leeds win the Second Division Championship, which marked the beginning of the most successful era in the club's history. In the next ten seasons with the Yorkshire giants Giles won a number of honours including League Championship medals in 1968/69 and 1973/74, an FA Cup winners' medal in 1971/72, a League Cup winners' medal in 1967/68 and UEFA Cup winners' medals in 1967/68 and 1970/71.

Giles made fifty-nine appearances for the Republic of Ireland, captaining his country a record thirty times. He became the youngest player to score for the Republic when he found the net just sixteen minutes into his debut against Sweden in November 1959, two months short of his twentieth birthday. His last game for Leeds was in the 1975 European Cup Final, which they lost 2–0 to the German champions Bayern Munich. The runners-up medal he collected after that game was only the second of his career; the other came when Leeds lost the 1965 FA Cup Final to Liverpool. His record in cup competitions is remarkable when one considers he played in eight finals.

In the summer of 1975, after playing in 527 League and Cup games for Leeds, he joined West Bromwich Albion. As player-manager of the Baggies, he took the club into the top flight at the end of his first season. After two seasons at The Hawthorns, he returned to Ireland to play for and manage Shamrock Rovers, guiding the club to victory in the 1978 FAI Cup.

Giles had been appointed player-manager of the Republic of Ireland in October 1973. He continued playing until May 1979 and then quit as manager the following March. Afterwards he had brief spells in management with Vancouver Whitecaps in 1983 and again at West Bromwich Albion in 1984/85. He eventually went into journalism and wrote a regular column in the *Daily Express* (indeed, he still writes for the paper periodically). He also works as a pundit for Irish television.

Johnny Giles shows his FA Cup winner's medal to his son (right) and his brother-in-law Nobby Stiles' son, 6 May 1972.

GEORGE GRAHAM
Midfielder
Born 30.11.44, Coatbridge

HONOURS
League Cup 1964/65
League Championship 1970/71
FA Cup 1970/71
Inter Cities Fairs Cup 1969/70
12 Scotland Caps

GEORGE GRAHAM was a Scottish Schoolboy and Youth international when he joined Aston Villa in December 1961. Although he spent three seasons at Villa Park, he failed to establish a regular place in the club's first team and in July 1964 Tommy Docherty signed him for Chelsea for a bargain £8,000. He made a promising start to his Chelsea career, scoring on his debut. Although he was no great runner and lacked pace, he proved to be a prolific marksman, finding the net seventeen times in thirty League appearances in 1964/65. The following season his total of twenty-three goals in all competitions was not bettered but the team that had brought Chelsea within touching distance of glory was breaking up amid mounting dressing-room disharmony.

Graham's transfer request was initially refused but, with the new campaign only six weeks old, he was allowed to join Arsenal in part-exchange for Tommy Baldwin. During his first two seasons at Highbury he was the Gunners' leading scorer, helping the club to League Cup Finals in 1967/68 and 1968/69. During this period Arsenal's backroom staff realised that George Graham's skills were being wasted as a centre-forward, so he was switched to a deeper position at inside-forward. This turned out to be a master stroke; not only did Arsenal win the Inter Cities Fairs Cup in 1969/70 but also the 'double' the following season. Graham won the first of his twelve Scottish caps in 1971/72 as well as helping Arsenal reach Wembley again the same season. However, after the arrival of Alan Ball, Graham's position in the Arsenal side was not certain and in December 1972 he was transferred to Manchester United for £120,000. He spent two years at Old Trafford before finishing his career with Portsmouth and Crystal Palace.

Graham later coached Crystal Palace and Queen's Park Rangers before being appointed manager of Millwall in December 1982. After saving the Lions from relegation to the Fourth Division in his first season at The Den, he guided the club to a Football League trophy win in 1983, followed by promotion to the Second Division in 1984/85. In May 1986 he was appointed manager of Arsenal and in his first season back at the club he guided the Gunners to a League Cup Final victory over Liverpool. In 1987/88 Arsenal were back at Wembley in the

same competition but lost to Luton Town. In 1988/89 Graham achieved his greatest success with Arsenal, winning the League Championship in the last minute of the final game against fellow contenders Liverpool. Arsenal repeated this feat with Championship title wins in 1990/91 and in 1992/93, when they became the first team ever to win the FA Cup and League Cup 'double'. In 1993/94 Arsenal beat Parma to lift the European Cup Winners' Cup, Graham writing himself into the record books as the first person to play for and manage European Cup winning sides.

In February 1995 he left Arsenal after speculation about transfer irregularities. He then took charge of Leeds United before leaving to manage Tottenham Hotspur. Graham, who was replaced by Glenn Hoddle in April 2001, is still out of the game, though his name is mentioned for every vacant managerial position!

EDDIE GRAY

Inside-Forward
Born 17.1.48, Belshill

LEAGUE RECORD

	A	G
Leeds United	442 (13)	52

HONOURS
League Cup 1967/68
League Championship 1968/69 and
 1973/74
FA Cup 1971/72
UEFA Cup 1967/68 and 1970/71
12 Scotland Caps

EDDIE GRAY was a most gifted and graceful player, but his career was plagued by a succession of injuries which would have prompted a lesser man to quit the game long before he did. Eddie Gray could confuse a full-back simply by dropping one of his hunched shoulders and feinting one way before dribbling off in the other direction!

A Scottish Schoolboy international, Eddie Gray joined Leeds United in January 1965, making his League debut a year later in a 3–0 home win over Sheffield Wednesday. His performances for the Elland Road club led to him winning two Under-23 caps for Scotland before he gained his full international spurs against England at Wembley. That came at the end of a season in which Leeds won the League Championship. The following year Eddie Gray gave a virtuoso performance in the FA Cup Final against Chelsea. However, after establishing himself as one of Scotland's most exciting post-war players, he ran into injury problems that threatened to end his career. He was written off by a number of people connected with the club but manager Jimmy Armfield was full of encouragement. He fought his way back to full fitness and during his rehabilitation he coached the Leeds' juniors. Although Gray had lost some of his speed, he staged a remarkable comeback in January 1974, when his ball skills were still very much in evidence.

Gray was still playing when he was appointed the club's player-manager in July 1982 in succession to Allan Clarke. Though he had no managerial experience, he had impressed when coaching the juniors. He ended his playing days at left-back while at the same time bringing back Peter Lorimer as captain. Gray, who received an MBE for his services to football, was unable to win back Leeds' First Division place although they were promotion candidates for three successive seasons. In October 1985 Gray and his assistant Jimmy Lumsden were sacked – for Gray it ended a 22-year association with the club. The day after the shock news Leeds beat Middlesbrough with a Lorimer penalty as United fans demonstrated against Gray's dismissal.

Gray later joined his former team-mate David Harvey as a player for non-League Whitby Town but by the start of the 1986/87 season he was working as Middlesbrough's reserve and youth team coach. In December 1986 he was appointed Rochdale's team manager before leaving to take charge of Hull City in the summer of 1988. After just one season at Boothferry Park he was sacked and returned to Whitby Town but quit in 1990 to concentrate on outside business interests. He returned to Leeds United in March 1995 as junior coach when Howard Wilkinson was manager and was appointed assistant-manager of Leeds United in October 1998 when David O'Leary took over the reins.

LEAGUE RECORD

	A	G
Chelsea	157	124
Tottenham Hotspur	321	220
West Ham United	36 (2)	13

HONOURS
FA Cup 1961/62
European Cup Winners' Cup 1962/63
57 England Caps

JIMMY GREAVES
Inside-Forward
Born 20.2.40, East Ham

JIMMY GREAVES was without doubt the greatest goalscorer in Spurs' history and arguably the history of British football. He made his Football League debut for Chelsea against Spurs on the opening day of the 1957/58 season. He scored then in a 1–1 draw, as he did on all his debut days. It was the first of 357 goals in the Football League, all of them in the First Division. After only six League games for Chelsea he made his debut for the England Under-23s and scored twice against Bulgaria at Stamford Bridge. He stayed with Chelsea until the summer of 1961 when he left to join AC Milan. He had actually signed a contract nine months earlier, but it was subject to the Italians lifting an embargo on foreign players. His full England debut and first international goal had come in a 4–1 defeat in Peru in May 1959. His goalscoring debut for Milan came in a friendly match against Botafoga. Despite the tough defensive tactics of the Italian League, he scored nine goals in fourteen matches, but he was not able to stomach the petty disciplines the Italians imposed on their players and made clear his desire to return to English football.

In December 1961 he joined Spurs for £99,999 – as Bill Nicholson refused to pay a six-figure fee! He responded on his debut with a hat-trick at home to Blackpool, starting with a superb scissors-kick. He won an FA Cup winners' medal in his first season, scoring the opening goal at Wembley. He scored twice in the European Cup Winners' Cup final the following year and ended the 1962/63 season as Spurs' then highest scorer-in-a-season with thirty-seven League goals. When he topped the First Division scoring chart in 1964/65 he became the first player to do so for three consecutive seasons. A serious illness in 1965/66 meant that he was unable to reach full fitness for the World Cup finals that summer. In his time with Spurs he won forty-two caps and scored twenty-eight goals – his overall record being forty-four goals in fifty-seven appearances.

In March 1970 he left Spurs to join West Ham United as part of the deal that took Martin Peters to White Hart Lane. He scored twice on his debut for the

FACT

While with Chelsea Jimmy Greaves became the youngest player to score a hundred Football League goals when he reached his ton against Manchester City on 19 November 1960, aged 20 years and 261 days.

Hammers but retired at the end of the 1970/71 season, when still only thirty-one years old. In October 1972 a crowd of 45,799 turned out at White Hart Lane to pay tribute in his testimonial match against Feyenoord. He responded in the only way he knew, scoring after only three minutes! He later played non-League football but fell victim to alcoholism, a problem that threatened his very existence. Rehabilitation was followed by new stardom as a television pundit, a role in which he revels.

RON HARRIS
Defender
Born 13.11.44, Hackney

LEAGUE RECORD

	A	G
Chelsea	646 (9)	13
Brentford	60 (1)	0

HONOURS
League Cup 1964/65
FA Cup 1969/70
European Cup Winners' Cup 1970/71

RON HARRIS had already made a handful of Football League appearances for Chelsea when he captained the England youth team that won the Little World Cup at Wembley in April 1963. Blues' manager Tommy Docherty was impressed by the eighteen-year-old's fierce will to win and decided that he was just the player to add resolve to the club's faltering promotion drive. Restored to the Chelsea defence four days later for the match against Preston North End, which the Blues won 2–0, he stayed there for the next seventeen years!

'Chopper' Harris was undoubtedly at his best playing alongside the centre-half, close marking the opposition's most dangerous forward. Even star players like George Best and Geoff Hurst rarely prospered when marked by Harris and former Chelsea favourite Jimmy Greaves, one of the game's most prolific goalscorers, only netted one in over twenty games against a Chelsea side that contained Ron Harris. In fact, Greavsie was heard to mutter why Spurs had even bothered to pick him for the games against Chelsea!

A most adaptable player, Harris was switched to full-back on a number of occasions because of injuries but this willingness to play out of position for the good of the team did little to advance his own career. In January 1966 Ron Harris replaced Terry Venables as Chelsea captain and led the club to four major finals: in 1970 the Blues won the FA Cup and the following year the European Cup Winners' Cup.

After the club's defeat by Stoke City in the 1972 League Cup Final, Harris found himself dropped from the side and though he later returned to the team he found the captaincy handed to Eddie McCreadie. Towards the end of his career at Stamford Bridge, manager Geoff Hurst asked him to play in midfield. His outstanding displays left one wondering what he might have achieved if he had played in this position a decade earlier. However, Harris and Hurst didn't always see eye to eye and in the close season, after having played in 794 games for Chelsea, Harris joined Brentford as the Griffin Park club's player-coach. In 1984/85 Harris took charge of Aldershot but lost his job at the end of a campaign in which the Shots finished fourteenth, when a new board took over the club. On leaving the Recreation Ground, he bought Bramhill Golf Club in Wiltshire but a few years later sold it for £2 million to golf professional Roger Mace and former Aldershot goalkeeper Glen Johnson. 'Chopper' now owns a holiday chalet and fishing complex in a most picturesque setting in a village near Warminster.

Ron Harris (right) and Willie Morgan.

LEAGUE RECORD

	A	G
Fulham	594	146

HONOURS
56 England Caps

JOHNNY HAYNES
Inside-Forward
Born 17.10.34, Edmonton

JOHNNY HAYNES was the country's first £100-a-week player; he was one of the first to use his fame for advertising and to have an agent; and he was captain of England on twenty-two occasions. Born and raised in Edmonton, he should have joined Spurs but after playing for England Schoolboys he chose Fulham. When Fulham won promotion to the First Division in 1958/59, Haynes was the club's leading scorer with twenty-six goals in thirty-four games, including hat-tricks in the wins over Sunderland (Home 6–2), Leyton Orient (Away 5–2) and Rotherham United (Home 4–0).

In 1961, after former Fulham colleague Jimmy Hill had secured the removal of the £20 maximum wage, club chairman Tommy Trinder declared that 'Johnny is worth £100 a week' and within twenty-four hours the negotiations for a revision of his contract were complete. Haynes gained his greatest satisfaction from his career with England, for whom he won fifty-six caps. He scored a hat-trick in a 5–0 win over Russia at Wembley in 1958 but without doubt his best game in England colours was the 9–3 defeat of Scotland in 1961. In August 1962, soon after several poor displays in the disappointing World Cup in Chile, Haynes was involved in a car crash in Blackpool. It was to end his international career and put his whole playing future in jeopardy. Then aged twenty-nine, he did not play for a year and was even told by doctors that he would never play again. Determined to prove them wrong, he worked hard and eventually regained full fitness.

The only time it looked at all possible for Haynes and Fulham to part company came after the tragic death of Spurs' Scottish international inside-forward John White in 1964. Bill Nicholson offered £90,000 for his services – it would have been a record fee between British clubs – but the deal did not go through. Considering his role as leader of men with Fulham and England, it is strange that Haynes didn't go into management when his playing career ended. He took over Fulham for seventeen days when Bobby Robson was sacked but he told the Fulham directors that he was not interested and he soon drafted in Bill Dodgin as coach and stood down in favour of him as manager. When he left the Cottagers in 1970, many people expected him to join Jimmy Hill as a television personality but instead he moved to South African football where he won his first honour – as a member of the Durban City side that clinched the League title. Haynes, the King of Craven Cottage, now resides in Edinburgh, where he runs a very successful dry-cleaning business.

KEVIN HECTOR
Forward
Born 2.11.44, Leeds

LEAGUE RECORD

	A	G
Bradford Park Avenue	176	113
Derby County	478 (8)	155

HONOURS
League Championship 1971/72 and 1974/75
2 England Caps

After trials with Hull City, Doncaster Rovers and Wolves, KEVIN HECTOR was playing for South Leeds when he was spotted by Bradford Park Avenue manager Jimmy Scoular, who signed him in 1962. His first few games were as a winger, but he soon switched to his best position at inside-forward. He made his League debut against Bournemouth and until his transfer to Derby County in September 1966 he scored 113 League goals in 176 consecutive appearances, topping the club's goalscoring charts in each season. In the 1965/66 season alone he scored sixty-four goals, including five in one 28-minute spell in a 7–2 win against Barnsley, which also produced a hat-trick in the space of nine minutes.

Everyone expected Hector to join Manchester City, but it was lowly Second Division club Derby County who took the gamble and they were fully rewarded as he became an instant success. He was the club's leading scorer in each of his first three seasons with the Rams, helping them win promotion to the top flight in 1968/69. He played a major part in the Derby side that won the League Championships as the Rams swept all before them. In setting a total of 589 appearances for Derby in all matches, he created a club record which is unlikely to be broken, and it was regarded as extraordinary by all those who saw him that

he made only two appearances for England, both times as substitute. His goalscoring ability was never open to question – during the 1976/77 UEFA Cup competition, he netted five of Derby's goals in a 12–0 win over Finn Harps!

Tommy Docherty sold Hector to Vancouver Whitecaps and he spent the English seasons playing for Boston United and Burton Albion before he was brought back to Derby by Colin Addison in 1980. He continued where he had left off, finally finishing his Football League career in May 1982. One of only a few players to score over a hundred League goals for two separate clubs, Kevin Hector now works as a postman in the East Midlands.

TERRY HENNESSEY
Midfielder
Born 1.9.42, Llay

LEAGUE RECORD

	A	G
Birmingham City	178	3
Nottingham Forest	159	5
Derby County	62 (1)	4

HONOURS
League Cup 1962/63
League Championship 1971/72
39 Wales Caps

TERRY HENNESSEY made five hundred senior appearances with three clubs: Birmingham City, Nottingham Forest and Derby County. He also won thirty-nine full caps for Wales and skippered his country and each of his League clubs. A Welsh Schoolboy international, Hennessey joined the Blues as an amateur in the summer of 1957, turning professional on his seventeenth birthday. Coached by former manager Pat Beasley, Hennessey was given his League debut by City's new boss Gil Merrick against Manchester City in March 1961, a match the Blues won 3–2. By the early part of the following season Hennessey had established himself as a regular member of the Birmingham midfield and in 1962/63 he won a League Cup winners' tankard and was voted Midlands 'Footballer of the Year'. Although he didn't score many goals, the defensive midfielder was at his best when winning the ball and striding forward looking to set up a counter-attack.

In November 1965 Hennessey was transferred to Nottingham Forest for £70,000 as the replacement for the long-serving Jeff Whitefoot. He made his League debut for his new team in a 2–1 home win over Blackpool when both Forest's goals were scored by the opposition! He was only twenty-three when he arrived at the City Ground, but looked much older because of his receding hairline. Showing great maturity in his play, he was appointed the club's captain and in 1966/67 led Forest to the runners-up spot in the First Division and to the FA Cup semi-finals where they lost 2–1 to Tottenham Hotspur. One of a number of players Forest manager Matt Gillies allowed to leave the City Ground, Hennessey joined Derby County in February 1970 as Dave Mackay's replacement.

Brian Clough made Hennessey Derby's first £100,000 signing and he played in the Rams' 1971/72 League Championship winning side, although his later career was dogged by injury. He left the Baseball Ground in May 1973 to become manager of Tamworth and later coached Kimberley Town and Shepshed Charterhouse. He was assistant-manager of Tulsa Roughnecks and assistant-coach to Alan Hinton at Vancouver Whitecaps in the NASL. He then emigrated to Australia where he became manager-coach of the Victoria State side, Heidelberg. Today, he lives just outside Melbourne and works as a sales manager for a local firm selling clingfilm products.

FREDDIE HILL

Inside-Forward
Born 17.1.40, Sheffield

LEAGUE RECORD

	A	G
Bolton Wanderers	373 (2)	74
Halifax Town	25	3
Manchester City	28 (7)	3
Peterborough United	73 (2)	7

HONOURS
2 England Caps

Emerging from junior football in his home city of Sheffield, FREDDIE HILL signed for Bolton Wanderers in 1957. He had already turned down an offer from Sheffield Wednesday in the hope of getting regular first-team football with the Trotters. He made his League debut for the Wanderers in April 1958 at the age of eighteen, as a replacement for the injured Dennis Stevens in a 1–1 draw against Newcastle United at Burnden Park.

When Nat Lofthouse retired Dennis Stevens replaced him at centre-forward, allowing Freddie Hill to become a permanent member of the attack at inside-forward. He had already begun to show his goalscoring ability when he netted seven goals from his eighteen appearances in 1958/59. On 4 March 1959 he scored the first of his two hat-tricks for the Wanderers in a 6–0 mauling of Chelsea and in 1961/62 he had his best season to date in terms of goals scored, netting fourteen in forty-one games.

FACT

In August 1962 Reading's goalkeeper Arthur Wilkie injured a hand during the match against Halifax Town. He came out of goal to play as a striker and scored twice in a 4–2 win.

After only three seasons in League football his ability was recognised when he was selected for the England Under-23 side. In October 1962 he was chosen to play in his first full international against Northern Ireland in Belfast. The following month he played against Wales at Wembley but it proved to be his last appearance in an England shirt.

During the 'Modern Ice Age' season of 1962/63 Bolton's third-round FA Cup tie against Sheffield United at Bramall Lane was finally played at the thirteenth attempt but the Wanderers lost 3–1. There was immediate revenge, however, for Freddie Hill hit his second hat-trick to secure the points against the Blades in Bolton's first home League game for three months! Between 1962 and 1964 Freddie Hill asked for a move on four occasions. His last request was accepted with great regret, for he was a firm favourite with the Burnden faithful. Liverpool were set to pay £60,000 for him, but withdrew their offer after Hill failed a medical because of high blood pressure.

The 1964/65 season was Hill's best in terms of goals scored, the scheming inside-forward netting fifteen times. He played for the Wanderers until the end of the 1968/69 campaign, scoring seventy-nine goals in 412 games. He left Bolton to join Halifax Town but within a year he was back in the top flight with Manchester City. At Maine Road he teamed up with Francis Lee and Wyn Davies to revive old Bolton partnerships. In August 1973 Hill moved to Peterborough United where he ended his League career. Now living in Peterborough, where he runs a town centre public house, this popular player was granted a late but thoroughly deserved testimonial when Bolton entertained Manchester City in October 1990.

JOHN HOLLINS

Midfielder
Born 16.7.46, Guildford

LEAGUE RECORD

	A	G
Chelsea	465	48
Queen's Park Rangers	148 (3)	6
Arsenal	123 (4)	9

HONOURS
League Cup 1964/65
FA Cup 1969/70
Second Division Championship 1983/84
1 England Cap

JOHN HOLLINS comes from a footballing family, with three of his brothers, his father and grandfather having played League football. He was one of a stream of good young players to emerge from the Stamford Bridge assembly line. He was neat and precise and made an impression at Chelsea in the early 1960s. His dynamic displays earned him a place in the England side that faced Spain at Wembley in May 1967, four days after he had played there for the Blues in the FA Cup Final, but that was to be his only appearance in a full international. After a couple of spells at right-back, when he was unable to reclaim his usual place from Peter Osgood after he had been sidelined by injury, he appeared to have lost much of his old zest but bounced back to play the best football of his career. He was voted the fans' 'Player of the Year' for two seasons in succession and in five seasons missed just four games. This was as a result of an ankle ligament injury in April 1971 that also caused him to miss the European Cup Winners' Cup replay against Real Madrid in Athens. He also scored many memorable goals for the Blues, none better than a spectacular solo effort against Arsenal in August 1970, while his venomously struck penalties helped him to a total of eighteen goals in all competitions in 1971/72.

At the start of the 1974/75 season Hollins was handed the club captaincy but, with the team struggling, new manager Eddie McCreadie left him out of the side and in the close season he followed Dave Sexton to Queen's Park Rangers. In his first season at Loftus Road, he helped the club to the runners-up spot in the First Division. He served Rangers well for another four seasons before surprisingly joining Arsenal. He was signed originally as a defensive cover player but settled into the team as a full-back (although occasionally reverting back to his old position of wing-half). He was still playing well at the age of thirty-six when Arsenal granted him a free transfer in May 1983. After twenty consecutive seasons of playing in the First Division he rejoined Chelsea to taste Second Division football for the first time.

FACT

In 1968/69 Rochdale fans were voted the best-behaved spectators in Division Four. A few days later the FA ordered the club to post warning notices on the ground after some fans had thrown objects on to the pitch.

In his first season Hollins helped Chelsea win promotion to the First Division. He retired at the end of the 1983/84 season, to be appointed team coach and manager in June 1985. Hollins, who was awarded the MBE for his services to football, was not popular with Chelsea fans because his teams tended to be efficient but dull! He resigned in March 1988 and after a spell as a financial adviser he was appointed manager of Swansea City. In his first season at The Vetch, he led the Swans to the play-offs, while in 1999/2000 the club won the Third Division Championship. Sadly, they were relegated after just one season of Second Division football and Hollins parted company with the club. He is now manager of Rochdale, which he took to the Third Division play-offs in 2001/02.

EDDIE HOPKINSON

Goalkeeper
Born 29.10.35, Wheatley Hill, Durham

LEAGUE RECORD

	A	G
Oldham Athletic	3	0
Bolton Wanderers	519	0

HONOURS
FA Cup 1957/58
14 England Caps

EDDIE HOPKINSON was only sixteen years of age when he played in three games for Oldham Athletic during the course of the 1951/52 season. In the summer months he played cricket for Royton in the Central Lancashire League and, until football stopped him, he was a county-level water-polo player. At the end of the 1951/52 season the Latics overlooked him, to Bolton's lasting satisfaction. He joined the Wanderers in August 1952, signing professional forms the following November. Over the next couple of years he played little football for Bolton as he was stationed in Scotland for his National Service.

Hopkinson's meteoric rise began in August 1956 when Bolton's regular keeper, Ken Grieves, the Lancashire cricketer, couldn't be released from his cricketing duties as Lancashire were chasing Championship honours. Eddie got his chance in the senior side against Blackpool and went through a brilliant first season without missing a game. At 5ft 9in, he was one of the smallest goalkeepers in the First Division. In the summer of 1957 he was awarded the first of six England Under-23 caps on a tour behind the Iron Curtain. In October of that year he made his first full international appearance against Northern Ireland, going on to play against all three countries in the Home Internationals and eventually collecting fourteen caps. In 1958 he kept a clean sheet to win an FA Cup winners' medal as the Wanderers beat Manchester United 2–0 at Wembley.

At Norwich City in January 1969 he broke Bolton's long-standing appearance record set by Alex Finney. Hopkinson played in 578 matches for Bolton and, but for an injury which kept him out of the side for most of the 1958/59 season and another which put him out of action for a ten-match spell in the 1963/64 season, he would have passed Finney's record much earlier. Professionals reckon that consistency is the true test of the top-class player and there were certainly few to rival Eddie Hopkinson in this aspect of his game. He remained Bolton's first-choice goalkeeper until the middle of the 1969/70 season when injury forced his retirement. He became assistant-trainer at Burnden Park, coaching both the youth and reserve sides. In July 1974 he left to join Stockport County as assistant-manager but his stay was brief.

He made an unexpected comeback when he volunteered to keep goal for the team he managed, Ashton United, after four players failed to show up for the Cheshire League game at Witton. Witton won 7–0 but 'Hoppy' got a great ovation as he retired at half-time to make way for the latecomers. In 1979 he returned to Bolton as goalkeeping coach but eventually left the game to become a representative for a chemical company. After working for a spell as a customer relations officer for Warburtons Bakery, Eddie Hopkinson, now retired, helps out at the Reebok Stadium on match days.

'ERNIE' HUNT

Inside-Forward
Born 17.3.43, Swindon

LEAGUE RECORD

	A	G
Swindon Town	214	82
Wolves	74	32
Everton	12 (2)	3
Coventry City	140 (6)	45
Doncaster Rovers	9	1
Bristol City	9 (3)	2

ROGER ('ERNIE') HUNT was working for British Rail when Swindon Town manager Bert Head signed him as an amateur in 1957. After working his way up through the ranks, Hunt made his League debut in September 1959, and then topped the club's scoring charts for the next four seasons. Hunt's best season in terms of goals scored was in 1962/63 as the Robins won promotion to the Second Division. His total of twenty-four League goals included a hat-trick in a 5–1 defeat of Brighton and Hove Albion. He was the club's leading scorer again in 1963/64 and early the following season netted his second hat-trick for the Robins in a 4–2 home win over Derby County. With the Wiltshire club, Hunt won three England Under-23 caps and scored eighty-two goals in 214 League games before signing for Wolverhampton Wanderers in September 1965.

He should have made his debut for Wolves at Southampton but he decided that he wasn't fully match fit and watched from the stands as the Saints won 9–3! He did make his debut in the next match, however, creating goals for Knowles, Wagstaffe and Wharton in a 3–0 home win over Bury. The following season he helped Wolves win promotion to the First Division, top-scoring with twenty goals in thirty-seven games, including a hat-trick in a 4–0 win at Northampton Town.

FACT

In the 1962 clash between Coventry City and Southend United the referee stopped the game after three minutes because both sides were wearing blue. He made the Sky Blues go back into the dressing-room and change into red.

Hunt, who had an excellent scoring record for a midfielder, had found the net thirty-five times in eighty-two outings for Wolves before joining Everton for £80,000.

Unable to settle at Goodison Park, he signed for Coventry City, making his debut for the Sky Blues in a 2–0 home win over Manchester United. At Highfield Road he teamed up with Willie Carr, the two of them perfecting the infamous 'donkey kick' which resulted in a spectacular goal on 'Match of the Day' as City beat League Champions Everton 3–1. On leaving Coventry, Hunt, who had already had a loan spell with Doncaster Rovers, joined Bristol City. Though he helped his new club beat Leeds United in the 1973/74 FA Cup fifth-round replay, his stay at Ashton Gate was brief and in November 1974 he left to play non-League football for Atherstone Town. He later played for Ledbury Town, where he also ran the Full Pitcher public house, and after hanging up his boots he taught in a children's home. There followed spells working in the commercial department of both Gloucester City and Swindon Town before he became a window cleaner. A hip injury now prevents him from working.

ROGER HUNT
Forward
Born 20.7.38, Golborne

LEAGUE RECORD

	A	G
Liverpool	401 (3)	245
Bolton Wanderers	72 (4)	24

HONOURS
Second Division Championship
  1961/62
League Championship 1963/64 and
  1965/66
FA Cup 1964/65
34 England Caps

Spotted by former Liverpool and England centre-half Bill Jones, ROGER HUNT had trials with Bury and Crewe before Liverpool signed him from Stockton Heath on amateur forms in 1958. He turned professional after completing his National Service and made his League debut as a 21-year-old against Scunthorpe United in September 1959, scoring in a 2–0 win. He ended the season with twenty-one goals in thirty-six games. In 1961/62 he helped shoot the Reds into Division One with forty-one goals from forty-one games, as he struck up a prolific partnership with Ian St John, thereby beating Gordon Hodgson's club record set in 1930/31.

In 1965/66, the season of their second title triumph, the Reds didn't lose any First Division game in which Hunt scored. On 6 September 1965 he hit a hat-trick in the space of seven minutes as Liverpool beat West Ham United 5–1. It was certainly no coincidence that Liverpool won the Championship in Hunt's two most prosperous seasons. His emergence as one of the top scorers in the country earned him a place in Alf Ramsey's squad of twenty-two for the 1966 World Cup Finals. Hunt kept Jimmy Greaves out of the line-up and scored three goals, playing in all six games. It was yet another unforgettable season for Hunt, with a World Cup winners' medal, a League Championship medal and an FA Cup Winners' Cup medal. The Anfield fans were not slow to recognise the part Hunt played and christened him 'Sir Roger'. However, although goalscoring was his forte, there was more to Roger Hunt. He had an explosive shot, and sudden and destructive pace with a phenomenal work-rate. He also possessed neat distribution, good ball control and a good footballing brain. He scored some spectacular goals, including a superb volley that he blasted into the Inter Milan net during the 1965 European Cup semi-final at Anfield. An even-tempered man, Hunt only once lost his temper on the field: in March 1969 he was substituted in an FA Cup defeat by Leicester City and hurled his shirt into the dug-out in frustration!

Earlier that season Bolton Wanderers had made moves to sign him but Hunt, who had supported the Trotters as a boy, refused to leave Anfield. However, in December 1969 the striker was persuaded to join the Wanderers in a £32,000 deal. In an eleven-season career at Anfield he had won two League Championship medals, a Second Division medal and an FA Cup winners' medal as well as scoring an astonishing 285 goals in all competitions for Liverpool. Unfortunately he could do little to revive the Wanderers' fortunes, though he did score a hattrick in a 3–0 win over Birmingham City as Bolton were relegated to the Third Division for the first time in their history.

In April 1972 over 56,000 attended his testimonial at Anfield to bid farewell to one of Liverpool's favourite sons and all-time great goalscorers. Since hanging up his boots, Hunt, who has been a member of the Pools Panel since 1974, has run his own haulage business near Merseyside.

NORMAN HUNTER
Central Defender
Born 29.10.43, Gateshead

LEAGUE RECORD

	A	G
Leeds United	540	18
Bristol City	108	4
Barnsley	28 (3)	0

HONOURS
Second Division Championship 1963/64
League Cup 1967/68
League Championship 1968/69 and 1973/74
FA Cup 1971/72
Inter Cities Fairs Cup 1967/68 and 1970/71
28 England Caps

NORMAN 'Bite yer legs' HUNTER was one of the game's fiercest competitors. The Leeds United defender, renowned for his tough tackling, relished the awesome reputation that often disguised the fact that he was an excellent footballer.

A former electrical fitter, Hunter turned professional with the Elland Road club in April 1961. He progreesed rapidly through the ranks and made his League debut against Swansea in September 1962. His outstanding performances at the heart of the Leeds' defence led to him winning three England Under-23 caps before he made his full international debut against West Germany in September 1966. Shortly afterwards he became the first England player to be capped as a substitute when he played against Spain. He went on to make twenty-eight full international appearances for his country, and it was only the presence of England captain Bobby Moore that prevented him from earning more international honours.

Norman Hunter was remarkably consistent, playing in every match for five seasons and featured in all Leeds United's Cup Finals from 1965 to 1975, finishing with two League Championship medals, an FA Cup winners' medal, a League Cup winners' medal and two Inter Cities Fairs Cup winners' medals. In 1974, he was voted the PFA's first-ever 'Player of the Year'.

In October 1976 Hunter, who had appeared in 725 League and Cup games for United, joined Bristol City for a fee of £40,000. He soon became a firm favourite at Ashton Gate, and was a key figure in the club's First Division survival fight. He was twice voted the Robins' 'Player of the Year' but he left Ashton Gate in the summer of 1979 when he was appointed player-coach at Barnsley under Allan Clarke. When Clarke left for Leeds in September 1980, Hunter took over at Oakwell and steered them into Division Two. He was surprisingly axed in February 1984 and then had a spell as assistant-manager at West Bromwich Albion before going to Rotherham United as manager in June 1985. He was dismissed in December 1987 and joined the coaching staff at Leeds in February 1988 but lost his job in October that year when Howard Wilkinson became manager.

Hunter became assistant to Terry Yorath at Bradford City in February 1989 but was sacked some twelve months later. He spent some time helping run a property business with his wife Suzanne and today he earns his living as an after-dinner speaker and as a summariser of Leeds' matches on BBC Radio Leeds.

CHARLIE HURLEY
Centre-Half
Born 4.10.36, Cork

LEAGUE RECORD

	A	G
Millwall	105	2
Sunderland	357 (1)	23
Bolton Wanderers	41 (1)	3

HONOURS
40 Republic of Ireland Caps

A living legend, CHARLIE HURLEY was recently voted Sunderland's best-ever player!

Born in Cork, he came to England at the age of seven to live in Hornchurch. He was spotted by Millwall scout Bill Voisey while playing with Rainham Youth Centre and signed amateur forms with the club. He had also played for West Ham's colts team and had trials with Arsenal but neither club took him on. In October 1953 he signed professional forms for Millwall, then playing in the Third Division (South), and he made his League debut as a seventeen-year-old, ousting fellow Irishman Gerry Bowdler from the side. He held on to his place in the Millwall side for four seasons, during which he became something of a folk hero at The Den. He had made 105 League appearances for the Lions and had just won his first full cap for the Republic of Ireland in a World Cup qualifier against England when Sunderland paid £18,000 for his services in September 1957. His first game for the club could not have been worse as the Wearsiders lost 7–0 at Blackpool and Hurley put through his own goal! At the end of his first season at Roker Park Sunderland were relegated from Division One for the first time in their 79-year history. Over the next six seasons Charlie Hurley became the bedrock on which Sunderland rebuilt their team for their return to the top flight, achieving this goal in 1963/64 as runners-up to Leeds United. Known as 'King Charlie', he went on to play in 402 League and Cup games for the club, and though he only scored twenty-six goals most of them were crucial strikes, such as the all-important goal late on in the match against Norwich City in the fifth round of the FA Cup in February 1961. In the summer of 1969 Hurley was given a free transfer by the board as a thank-you for the loyal service he had shown while with the club. He was allowed to negotiate his own contract and he joined Bolton Wanderers.

Hurley captained the Republic of Ireland in twenty-one of his forty international appearances, also serving as coach in his last three games until Mick Meagan was appointed the country's first official manager in September 1969.

FACT

On 26 November 1966 David Herd scored against three different goalkeepers at Old Trafford when Manchester United beat Sunderland 5–0. He scored four times, the first against Jim Montgomery, the second against Charlie Hurley and the final two against John Parke.

After two seasons with the Trotters he was appointed manager of Reading and took them to promotion for the first time in fifty years when they finished third in Division Four in 1975/76. They were relegated the following year and Hurley resigned, saying that the players were not responding to his methods of management. Since leaving Elm Park Charlie has worked in his family packing business, where he is the sales manager.

LEAGUE RECORD

	A	G
West Ham United	410 (1)	180
Stoke City	103 (5)	30
West Bromwich Albion	10	2

HONOURS

FA Cup 1963/64
European Cup Winners' Cup 1964/65
49 England Caps

GEOFF HURST's first football headline came when he was fined £1.50 for playing football in the streets, but by the time his playing career was over the Lancashire-born striker had made many more headlines for better reasons. The son of Charlie Hurst, a former professional with Oldham, Bristol Rovers and Rochdale, Geoff won six youth international caps in 1959 before making his League debut for West Ham United at Nottingham Forest in February 1960. At this time he was a dogged wing-half and little more. Indeed, he had become so disillusioned with his lack of progress that he was ready for a change of clubs. West Ham's manager Ron Greenwood saw in Hurst the strength of character and the eagerness to learn needed for the tactical revolution he was about to undertake. Greenwood wanted a forward with brains and vision to be a mobile target for passes from defence, to be an elusive, unpredictable 'wall' off which attacks could be built in the opponents' half and then to be the unfindable, unmarkable late-arriving finisher, who would sweep in on goal to deliver the ultimate shot.

FACT

On 15 November 1969 West Ham United featured in the first-ever English football match to be televised in colour . . . unfortunately hardly anyone had colour televisions, so most people saw it in black and white anyway.

Hurst played his first game at inside-left at home to Liverpool in September 1962. In 1963/64, his first full season in his new position, he netted twenty-six League and Cup goals, including the Hammers' second in the 3–2 FA Cup Final win over Preston North End. Yet Hurst was few people's idea of a good player; as late as January 1966 he was still being barracked by a section of the Upton Park crowd.

One important man shared Greenwood's perception: Alf Ramsey. In the 1965/66 season, in which Hurst scored forty goals in fifty-nine games, he was selected for England for the first time. Though he had to suffer the torment of sitting on the sidelines to watch England struggle through the first three matches of the World Cup finals without him, he came into the team for the quarter-final and scored the only goal in the game against Argentina. In the final he demonstrated his all-round talent with three goals in the 4–2 extra time win over West Germany – one with his head, one with his right foot and the last with his left.

Hurst's equanimity during those punishing years bordered on the miraculous. In 1968/69 he scored twenty-nine League goals, six of them in one game against

Sunderland, ending the season with forty-one League and Cup goals in forty-nine games. He played in 499 games for the Hammers, scoring 248 goals before joining Stoke City ahead of the 1972/73 season. He spent three seasons at the Victoria Ground before moving on to end his League career at West Bromwich Albion. After a season in the United States with Seattle Sounders, he became player-manager of Telford United before moving into full-time management with Chelsea. In 1981 he left Stamford Bridge to work in the insurance business, and is now the managing director of a company selling car warranties.

JOHN JACKSON
Goalkeeper
Born 5.9.42, Hammersmith

LEAGUE RECORD

	A	G
Crystal Palace	346	0
Leyton Orient	226	0
Millwall	79	0
Ipswich Town	1	0
Hereford United	4	0

JOHN JACKSON joined Crystal Palace in March 1962 and worked his way up through the ranks before making his Football League debut as Bill Glazier's deputy at Swindon Town in the second game of the 1964/65 season. In mid-October Coventry City swooped to take Glazier to Highfield Road for £35,000, a record fee for a goalkeeper. Palace manager Dick Graham went back to his former club West Bromwich Albion to buy Welsh international keeper Tony Millington but by the turn of the year Jackson had replaced the Welshman as the club's first-choice keeper.

Over the next four seasons Jackson was a model of consistency, with the highlight of his career coming in 1968/69 when he was ever-present in the Palace side that finished runners-up to Derby County in Division Two. In the top flight Jackson really came into his own, playing in 138 consecutive League games after his debut before illness in October 1972 forced him to miss the game at Wolverhampton Wanderers. During those matches it was Jackson's superb displays that salvaged precious points for the Eagles against the odds – points which at the end of the season made all the difference between relegation and survival.

In the end, though, not even John Jackson's heroics could keep Crystal

> **FACT**
>
> Crystal Palace played Real Madrid in a friendly at Selhurst Park on 18 April 1962 to inaugurate the club's new floodlighting system. Despite a day and a half of continual rain before the kick-off, a crowd of over 25,000 turned out to watch Real Madrid win 4–3. The Spanish team had agreed to play for a guaranteed fee of £10,000. Palace, who had increased admission charges on the night, took £15,000 in receipts and were able to show a profit of around £3,000 for the event.

Palace in the First Division. He had missed just four games in four seasons. Several top clubs might have been more tempted to buy him had he been a more acrobatic, headline-grabbing performer. As it was, he chose to go about his job quietly and effectively – but few goalkeepers have earned more respect and admiration than John Jackson did during his time in the top flight. He had the misfortune to be an outstanding goalkeeper in an age of great keepers – Gordon Banks, Peter Shilton and Ray Clemence to name but three – but even so he surely deserved more honours than his single appearance for the Football League.

Jackson was a surprise omission from the Palace side at the start of the 1973/74 season and though he later regained his place it wasn't long before he left

Selhurst Park to play for Leyton Orient. He spent six years at Brisbane Road without missing a game, which is a remarkable record. He then went to Millwall and was still playing at nearly forty years of age. It was at this stage of his career that he collected an unexpected bonus. Bobby Robson's Ipswich Town team was chasing the UEFA Cup in 1980/81 when they were suddenly hit by a series of injuries to their goalkeepers. Robson asked Jackson if he would like to travel to Widzew Lodz in Poland as goalkeeping cover. He went but wasn't needed – although it was his first and only taste of European football.

Now living in Brighton where he installs blinds, John Jackson was goalkeeping coach and youth development officer for the Seagulls until losing his job along with manager Steve Gritt in February 1998.

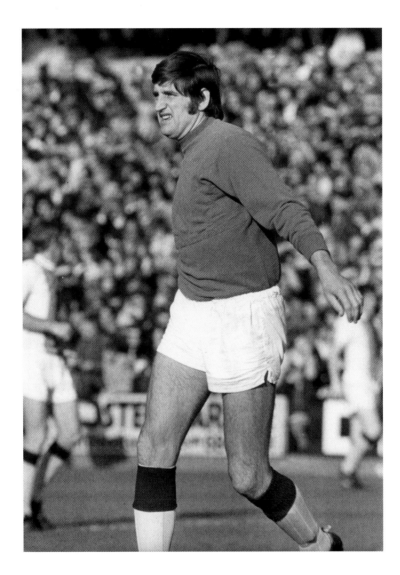

LEAGUE RECORD

	A	G
Watford	48	0
Tottenham Hotspur	472	0
Arsenal	237	0

HONOURS
FA Cup 1966/67 and 1978/79
League Cup 1970/71 and 1972/73
UEFA Cup 1971/72
European Cup Winners' Cup 1979/80
119 Northern Ireland Caps

PAT JENNINGS
Goalkeeper
Born 12.6.45, Newry

At his peak PAT JENNINGS was the best goalkeeper in the world and certainly a candidate for the best of all time. Having played Gaelic football for North Down Schools, he turned to football with Newry United, Newry Town's junior club. After a season with the juniors and six months with Newry Town, he joined Watford in the summer of 1963. A year later he was on his way to White Hart Lane as Spurs' boss Bill Nicholson paid Watford £27,000.

In a thirteen-year spell at Tottenham Jennings won an FA Cup winners' medal against Chelsea in 1967, two League Cup winners' medals against Aston Villa and Norwich City in 1971 and 1973 respectively, and a UEFA Cup winners' medal by beating Wolves in 1972. He was also the PFA 'Player of the Year' in 1976. He went on to set a record number of appearances for Spurs, a figure bettered only by Steve Perryman. He was awarded the MBE for his services to the game in the 1976 Queen's Birthday Honours list. His achievements were also honoured by Spurs with a testimonial game against Arsenal in November 1976. He was tough and rarely injured, but he did succumb to a serious ankle injury in 1976/77; during his enforced absence Spurs were relegated! Even worse, manager Keith Burkinshaw allowed Jennings to join rivals Arsenal, then managed by his former Spurs boss and international colleague Terry Neill. Jennings spent eight seasons at Highbury, making over three hundred senior appearances, winning another FA Cup winners' medal in 1979 and a European Cup Winners' Cup medal in 1980.

In the 1967 FA Charity Shield Pat Jennings scored a goal from his area against Manchester United: the longest-distance goal in the competition.

FACT

In May 1985 Jennings was granted a second testimonial, this time against Spurs. On the verge of retiring, he returned to White Hart Lane as goalkeeping cover for Ray Clemence and also to keep fit for Northern Ireland ahead of the 1986 World Cup Finals. He won another nine caps in his second spell with Spurs, giving him a world record total of 119. The conclusion of the World Cup saw Jennings officially retire, though later that year he did captain the Rest of the World XI against the Americas in a FIFA/UNICEF charity match. Since then the popular Irishman has shared his time between coaching the goalkeepers at White Hart Lane and making personal appearances.

CLIFF JONES
Winger
Born 7.2.35, Swansea

LEAGUE RECORD

	A	G
Swansea City	168	47
Tottenham Hotspur	314 (4)	135
Fulham	23 (2)	2

HONOURS
League Championship 1960/61
FA Cup 1960/61, 1961/62 and
  1966/67
European Cup Winners' Cup
  1962/63
59 Wales Caps

CLIFF JONES was one of Wales' greatest-ever players. He was the fourth member of his family to make his name in professional football, following his father Ivor, who played for Swansea Town, West Bromwich Albion and Wolves; his uncle Bryn, who played for Wolverhampton Wanderers, Arsenal, Norwich City and Wales; and his brother Bryn, who played for Swansea Town, Newport County, Bournemouth, Northampton Town and Watford.

After captaining the Swansea Schoolboys team that won the English Schools Shield for the second time since the war in 1949/50, Cliff Jones was taken on to the staff at the Vetch Field. However, he was wise enough to learn a trade outside football, becoming a sheet metal worker at Swansea Docks. He made his first-team debut for the Swans as a seventeen-year-old in October 1952 at inside-forward but was later persuaded by Swansea trainer Joe Sykes to switch to the wing. Jones never looked back, his form leading to him winning the first of fifty-nine caps for Wales when he played against Austria in May 1954. His performances for both club and country led to a number of top-flight clubs making inquiries about him but just when it seemed as if he would leave the Vetch he had to do his two years' National Service.

After returning to Swansea, Jones was eventually signed by Tottenham Hotspur, who, after a long series of negotiations, paid £35,000 to take him to White Hart Lane. After just three months with Spurs he was off to Sweden with Wales for the 1958 World Cup Finals.

On his return to White Hart Lane for pre-season training, Jones broke a leg in a practice game. It was a major blow for both player and club, although it did allow him to recharge his batteries. When he returned to first-team action four months later he became an indispensable member of the team, capable of playing on either wing or even at inside-forward. There were few more exciting sights in the game than to see Cliff Jones leave his marker for dead with a great burst of speed. Always alert to the possibility of cutting inside with the ball to shoot for goal, he was also an accomplished header. He was an important member of Spurs' 'double' winning team of 1960/61 and the team that won the FA Cup in 1962 and the European Cup Winners' Cup in 1963. Jones also picked up a third FA

Cup winners' medal in 1967 as the first non-playing substitute in an FA Cup Final. In October 1968 he was allowed to leave White Hart Lane to join Fulham but in two years at Craven Cottage he found himself occupying a completely different role from the one he had enjoyed at Spurs, a role that involved him doing more running!

After winding down his career with a number of non-League clubs he opened a butcher's shop in Tottenham High Road but unfortunately it wasn't a success and he returned briefly to the sheet metal trade he had learned as a sixteen-year-old. He then worked at a sports centre before becoming a games instructor at Highbury Grove School.

Now retired, Cliff Jones still helps out at Spurs' home games in their Legends Club.

MICK JONES
Centre-Forward
Born 24.4.45, Worksop

LEAGUE RECORD

	A	G
Sheffield United	149	63
Leeds United	215 (4)	77

HONOURS
League Championship 1968/69 and
   1973/74
FA Cup 1971/72
Inter Cities Fairs Cup 1967/68 and
   1970/71
3 England Caps

MICK JONES was an aggressive, non-stop, strong running centre-forward. His father had kept goal for Worksop but Mick soon developed the knack of scoring goals and once hit fourteen in a game for Priory Primary School! He played for Worksop Boys and Rotherham Boys and began work in a cycle factory while playing for Dinnington Miners' Welfare. He signed for Sheffield United in 1962 and made his League debut in a 1–1 draw at Manchester United in April 1963. Jones didn't score, but he netted twice in the next game as the Blades won 3–1 at Manchester City, finishing the season with four goals in seven games.

On Boxing Day 1963 United trailed 3–0 to Nottingham Forest after fifteen minutes but two goals from Mick Jones, the second in the very last minute of the games, helped the Blades to a 3–3 draw. Capped at Under-23 level, Jones, whose partnership in 1964/65 with Alan Birchenall gave opponents plenty of headaches, won his place in the full England side. His strong and purposeful all-round displays, coupled with his goalscoring feats – he was Sheffield United's top-scorer for three successive seasons – led to Leeds United paying £100,000 for his services in September 1967. Sheffield United manager John Harris said: 'It would be the biggest mistake the club had ever made allowing Jones to move.' At Elland Road, Jones's partnership with Allan Clarke proved a deadly formation and yet it was never tried at international level.

Jones won two League Championship medals in 1968/69 and 1973/74, an FA Cup winners' medal in 1972 (when he was injured and had to be led up to the royal box with his arm in a sling) and Inter Cities Fairs Cup winners' medals in 1968 and 1971. He also earned an England recall in 1970. Later he struggled with injuries and a serious knee problem ended his career in October 1975. He then became a representative for a sports goods company before running a sports shop in Maltby. Still living in his home town of Worksop, he now runs a market stall with his son, selling sportswear in Nottingham and South Yorkshire.

LEAGUE RECORD

	A	G
Preston North End	447	0

HONOURS

Third Division Championship 1970/71
47 Republic of Ireland Caps

ALAN KELLY

Goalkeeper
Born 5.7.36, Dublin

ALAN KELLY senior is the Republic of Ireland's second most capped goalkeeper after Celtic's Paddy Bonner. Only a serious injury in September 1973, in a game against Bristol City, prevented him from winning more caps. The father of Alan and Gary Kelly, goalkeepers currently with Blackburn Rovers and Oldham Athletic respectively, he grew up in County Wicklow, where his early promise was noted by the scouts attending schoolboy matches and he was snapped up by League of Ireland club Drumcondra. He won an FAI Cup winners' medal with the Drums when they defeated Shamrock Rovers 2–0 in the 1957 final. A year later, in April 1958, he moved to Preston North End.

Kelly had already made his international debut against West Germany when he suffered the traumatic experience of losing 5–1 to England in a World Cup tie at Wembley in May 1957. The goals against Ireland were not really Kelly's fault, as several outfield players 'seized up' on the big occasion. He had to wait almost five years, however, for his next cap. From then on his inspired displays made him a regular in the international side.

> **FACT**
>
> In the 1965/66 season Preston North End had sixteen Scottish-born players on their staff. In addition, manager Jimmy Milne was from Dundee and the reserve team trainer Willie Cunningham was born in Hill O' Beath. The club's principal Scottish scout was appropriately named Jimmy Scott!

Kelly had to wait until 1960/61 before breaking into the first team at Deepdale but when he did he showed what he could do in no uncertain manner. He replaced Fred Else, who had to miss the game through illness, in a fourth-round FA Cup tie against Swansea at the Vetch Field. He performed heroically during the ninety minutes, though any praise he received after the game was in stark contrast to his next game four days later. It was Kelly's League debut, the venue Hillsborough, home of Sheffield Wednesday – who thrashed North End 5–1.

Kelly soon put such disappointments to the back of his mind and went on to establish a League appearance record that still stands today. His consistency can be seen by the fact that in five successive seasons from 1966 he missed just 5 out of a possible 214 League games and he was never dropped. In thirteen seasons as a player at Deepdale he experienced all the trauma, exultation and drama normally associated with a top-flight club. He saw the club slide from a peak of second place in Division One in 1957/58 to Division Three at the end of the 1969/70 season. On the other hand they won the Third Division Championship the following season and were narrowly defeated 3–2 by West Ham in the 1964 FA Cup Final.

When his playing days ended Alan Kelly threw himself into the Deepdale club's administrative affairs before taking over as coach and assistant to Nobby Stiles. In 1983 he took over as Preston North End manager for a short spell. Later attached to the coaching staff at Everton, he now lives in Washington DC where he runs a number of goalkeeping clinics.

HOWARD KENDALL
Wing-Half
Born 22.5.46, Ryton-on-Tyne

LEAGUE RECORD

LEAGUE RECORD

	A	G
Preston North End	104	13
Everton	231 (2)	21
Birmingham City	115	16
Stoke City	82	9
Blackburn Rovers	79	6

HONOURS
League Championship 1969/70

HOWARD KENDALL was the youngest player ever to appear in an FA Cup Final when, at the age of seventeen years and 345 days, he played for Preston North End against West Ham United in 1964. In March 1967 Everton manager Harry Catterick paid North End £80,000 for the 21-year-old, and just two days after putting pen to paper he made his debut for the Toffees against Southampton. He went on to be part of one of the most influential midfield combinations that Everton have ever had. Along with Ball and Harvey, he helped the Blues to an emphatic Championship success in 1969/70. A wing-half from the old school, Kendall was a steady passer, defended well and made good forward runs but he didn't score many goals. He collected Football League representative honours and Under-23 caps and was unlucky not to get into the senior side. He was certainly good enough to have played for England, for at times his influence in midfield at Everton was quite awesome.

In February 1974 he was part of a complex transfer package which took Bob Latchford from Birmingham City to Everton while Kendall made the opposite journey. He proved a reliable buy for the St Andrew's club, helping to stabilise them in the First Division and also taking them to the 1975 FA Cup semi-finals.

In August 1977 Kendall joined Stoke City as club coach under Alan Durban as the Potters won promotion to Division One in

Gil Merrick was in charge of Birmingham City when they won the League Cup in the 1962/63 season – the only post-war occasion that a former goalkeeper has been manager of a Football League club which has achieved such an honour.

FACT

1978/79. In the close season he arrived at Blackburn Rovers as the club's player-manager. During his time at Ewood his brilliant performances on the field helped take the club from the Third Division to the brink of the First Division within two seasons. Despite entering the veteran stage of his career, he showed all the determination and drive of his earlier days, dictating play and inspiring those around him.

It was perhaps the least surprising event in his career when he returned to Goodison Park as player-manager in the summer of 1981. He had his problems in those early days but in 1983/84 the club won the FA Cup and reached the final of the League Cup. The following season Everton won the League Championship

and the European Cup Winners' Cup as well as reaching the FA Cup Final. Kendall was named Manager of the Year. After Everton won the League Championship in 1986/87, Kendall felt he could do no more at Goodison and was enticed to Athletico Bilbao in Spain. He has since managed Manchester City, Everton again, Notts County, Sheffield United and Everton for a third time, parting company with the club following a season in which they only held on to their premiership status on goal difference from Bolton Wanderers.

Kendall is now an after-dinner speaker.

LEAGUE RECORD

	A	G
Middlesbrough	37	0
Tottenham Hotspur	402 (1)	15

HONOURS
FA Cup 1966/67
League Cup 1970/71 and 1972/73
UEFA Cup 1971/72
4 England Caps

CYRIL KNOWLES
Left-Back
Born 13.7.44, Fitzwilliam
Died 13.8.91

CYRIL KNOWLES was born in the same mining village as England cricketer Geoff Boycott, and had a year on the junior staff at Manchester United before being rejected. There were further rejections from Blackpool and Wolves before Middlesbrough took him on their amateur staff. In those days Knowles was a winger but it wasn't long before he was converted into a full-back. His impressive displays soon had the top-flight clubs after his signature and in May 1964, after making just thirty-nine League and Cup appearances for Boro, he joined Tottenham Hotspur for a fee of £45,000.

In his first season at White Hart Lane he occupied the right-back position and represented England at Under-23 level before playing for Young England against England in the annual match on the eve of the FA Cup Final. He then moved across to left-back and over the next ten years the only games he missed were through injury. A member of the Spurs teams that won the FA Cup in 1967, the League Cup in 1971 and 1973 and the UEFA Cup in 1972, he won a total of six Under-23 caps, played for the Football League against the Scottish League in March 1968, represented England against Young England in both 1968 and 1969, and won four full caps, the first against Russia in December 1967.

A national cult figure because of the success of the pop record 'Nice One, Cyril', the title of which became a national catchphrase, Knowles was hugely popular with the Spurs fans. However, he suffered a serious knee injury towards the end of 1973. Although he recovered enough to help save the club from relegation in 1974/75, scoring two goals in the final match against Leeds United, the injury flared up again the following season and in the summer of 1976 news of his premature retirement was announced.

After his retirement he had a short spell as Hertford Town manager and then acted as a scout for Spurs. He worked as a coach with Doncaster Rovers and Middlesbrough until he was appointed assistant-manager at Ayresome Park. In May 1983 he took on the manager's job at Darlington, leading them to promotion from Division Four in 1984/85 but left in March 1987 when they were all but relegated. The following season he joined Torquay United, taking them to the Sherpa Van Trophy Final in 1989 before resigning in October of the same year. He was then appointed manager of Hartlepool United but in February 1991, with the club heading for promotion, he discovered he was suffering from a serious brain illness. He died just six months later.

BRIAN LABONE

Centre-Half
Born 23.1.40, Liverpool

LEAGUE RECORD

	A	G
Everton	451	2

HONOURS
League Championship 1962/63 and
 1969/70
FA Cup 1965/66
26 England Caps

One of the greatest players to wear the royal blue of Everton, BRIAN LABONE won every honour in the game, including twenty-six England caps, and he captained the club for seven years. He made his Everton debut at the age of eighteen in March 1958 when the Blues' regular centre-half Tommy Jones was injured. On his first appearance at Goodison Park he was given the run-around by Spurs' Bobby Smith as the Blues lost 4–3; deemed responsible for three of the goals, young Labone was dropped. Recalled midway through the following season, he went on to become one of the game's great competitors. He was only booked twice in 530 first-team appearances, despite playing against some of the roughest and toughest strikers in the country.

Labone won the first of his twenty-six England caps in October 1962 playing against Northern Ireland in Belfast. He was only twenty-two years old and was the first Everton player since the war to be capped – a great achievement. In 1966 he had a great chance of being picked as England's World Cup centre-half, but he made a shock request to be overlooked in order that he could go ahead with his planned summer marriage to a former Miss Liverpool. That news soon took a back seat as Labone fulfilled his boyhood dream and led the Blues to victory in the FA Cup Final against Sheffield Wednesday.

Just sixteen months after that Wembley success Labone dropped a bombshell by announcing his retirement. He revealed that he wasn't enjoying his football and would be quitting at the end of his contract (or earlier if Everton could find a replacement). Having made this announcement he began to produce some of his best-ever football and was recalled into the England squad. Some sixteen months later he announced he would be staying on to allow Everton to use his ability and experience to the full in a team of very promising youngsters. He was a key figure when the League Championship returned to Goodison in 1970. One of the greatest of club men, Labone was a pillar in the Everton defence for fifteen seasons. A great leader, he captained a Football League XI against the Irish and led an FA select side in Canada.

Brian Labone was one of the old school of footballers, surviving the football revolution to remain the model professional. He was finally forced to quit the game after an Achilles tendon injury. His loss was a shattering blow to Everton –

and one they would feel for the next decade. On leaving Everton, he went into an electrical contracting concern on Merseyside before working in the insurance industry. The call of football was too great, though, and he returned to Goodison Park to work in the club's commercial office.

DENIS LAW

Inside-Forward
Born 24.2.40, Aberdeen

LEAGUE RECORD

	A	G
Huddersfield Town	81	16
Manchester City	66 (2)	30
Manchester United	305 (4)	171

HONOURS
FA Cup 1962/63
League Championship 1964/65 and
  1966/67
55 Scotland Caps

DENIS LAW was one of the greatest strikers and characters in the modern game, yet when he arrived at Huddersfield Town from Aberdeen in 1956 he was a thin, bespectacled sixteen-year-old who looked nothing like a footballer. A year after joining Huddersfield, Law became the youngest player (at 18 years and 236 days) to represent Scotland in modern times when he made his debut against Wales. He stayed with the Yorkshire club until March 1960 when Manchester City paid Huddersfield £55,000 for his services. It was a League record, surpassing the previous British transfer record by £10,000. On 28 January 1961 Law produced the display of a lifetime to score six goals in a fourth-round FA Cup tie, only for the referee to abandon the game with twenty-one minutes to play! Luton Town were City's opponents at Kenilworth Road, racing into a two-goal lead within the first fifteen minutes. However, before half-time Law had completed his hat-trick and within twenty-five minutes of the second half he had collected his second hat-trick! His six goals had come in the space of forty-eight minutes but the conditions were worsening and the referee ended the game.

On 13 July 1961 Italian giants Torino paid £100,000 for Law's skills. It was the first time that a British club had been involved in a six-figure transfer. A year later he joined Manchester United when they became the first British club to pay over £100,000 for a player. He was worth the price. He was unselfish in setting up goals for team-mates, yet he had a killer instinct himself and in the six-yard box he was electric. He could score goals from impossible situations, and his blond hair and one arm raised to salute a goal helped establish the Law legend.

On 3 November 1962 he scored four goals for Manchester United against Ipswich and then four days later scored a further four goals for Scotland against Norway. A year earlier he had scored four goals for Scotland against Northern Ireland. Law rounded off a superb first season by scoring at Wembley in United's 3–1 FA Cup Final victory over Leicester City.

Denis Law holds the record for the most hat-tricks scored in European Cup competitions by anyone playing for a Football League club. Soon his goals (between lengthy bouts of suspension as he rebelled against the increasingly harsh treatment he was receiving from opposing defenders) were inspiring

United to two League Championships but unfortunately he had to watch United's 4–1 win over Benfica in the 1968 European Cup Final from his hospital bed after a knee operation. Though his disciplinary record prevented him from being voted 'Footballer of the Year', the English soccer writers' counterparts on the continent voted him 'European Footballer of the Year' in 1964. He enjoyed an Indian Summer with Manchester City as he returned to Maine Road in July 1973. Ironically his last League goal was a cheeky back-heel, which consigned United to the Second Division – never had he taken less pleasure from a goal.

Since retiring from football, Denis Law has worked as a commentator for both television and radio, and he is still a popular after-dinner speaker.

CHRIS LAWLER
Right-Back
Born 20.10.43, Liverpool

HONOURS
FA Cup 1964/65
League Championship 1965/66
  and 1972/73
UEFA Cup 1972/73
4 England Caps

CHRIS LAWLER, the man they called 'the Silent Knight', scored sixty-one goals for Liverpool in a playing career that spanned more than fourteen years. His ability to pop up in the opposition's penalty area and tuck the ball away made him one of the greatest full-backs in Liverpool's history. He became a regular choice in the Liverpool side in 1964/65 when he completed a successful season by winning an FA Cup winners' medal as the Reds beat Leeds United 2–1 after extra time.

Lawler was incredibly loyal to Liverpool and even postponed his wedding when the Reds played Inter Milan in the 1965 European Cup semi-final. A remarkable statistic concerning Chris Lawler was his eleven goals in sixty-six appearances in European football. One of the full-back's most inspired performances came against Honved of Hungary in the 1965/66 European Cup Winners' Cup. After a goalless draw in Hungary the Reds went all-out for an early goal in the return leg at Anfield. Lawler struck with a header after Peter Thompson had hit a post and then the full-back saw two great attempts strike the woodwork and he narrowly missed with two others. That season Lawler missed just two games through injury as Liverpool won the League Championship, one of his five goals coming after just twenty seconds in the 2–2 draw with Sunderland at Roker Park.

Lawler was chosen to play for England and made his international debut four days after appearing in the FA Cup Final against Arsenal in May 1971, playing against Malta in a European Championship qualifier. He scored in a 5–0 Wembley victory and went on to win three more caps, never playing on the losing side.

Lawler was ever-present in 1971/72 and again the following season when Liverpool won both the League Championship and the UEFA Cup. Sadly, a knee injury sustained at Loftus Road ended his proud record of consistency and despite a handful of appearances he was never the same again. After a move to Manchester City was called off by Liverpool at the last minute, Lawler was transferred to Portsmouth in October 1975. He ended his career with Stockport County.

After hanging up his boots, Lawler went back to Anfield and was a member of the famous bootroom, coaching the club's youngsters. However, during the reign of Kenny Dalglish Lawler left the club he had served so well. His coolness, control and attacking skills will long live on in the memories of Liverpool supporters.

LEAGUE RECORD

	A	G
Bolton Wanderers	189	92
Manchester City	248 (1)	112
Derby County	62	24

HONOURS

League Championship 1967/68 and
   1974/75
League Cup 1969/70
European Cup Winners' Cup 1969/70
27 England Caps

FRANCIS LEE

Forward
Born 29.4.44, Westhoughton, Bolton

FRANCIS LEE made his Football League debut for Bolton Wanderers as a 16-year-old amateur in November 1960, partnering 35-year-old Nat Lofthouse on the right wing in a 3–1 victory over Manchester City. It was an eventful debut for Lee as he scored a goal and got booked! His volatile nature caused problems off the field during his early days at Bolton when he refused to play after being dropped to the club's 'A' team. The situation was patched up and although several clubs were keen to sign him, following a string of transfer requests, Lee stayed with Bolton until the beginning of the 1967/68 season. It was then that he joined Manchester City and soon became a great favourite with the Maine Road fans. He was one of the successes in a City team that enjoyed one of the greatest eras in the club's history.

Francis Lee was a bustling, sturdy little striker. Barrel chested and rather portly, he was one of the most tenacious and effective of strikers, scoring many goals. He hit three hat-tricks in his time at Maine Road, including a spectacular threesome in the Manchester derby of 1970/71. His others came in the 5–2 defeat of Wolverhampton Wanderers in January 1972 and in a 4–0 home win over Walsall, in a League Cup second-round replay played at Old Trafford after the first two matches hadn't produced a goal.

Francis Lee scored a lot of penalties for City and wasn't really fussy *how* he scored them. In the European Cup Winners' Final of 1970, he hit the ball so hard and straight into the net that it needed a close study of an action-replay to be sure the ball hadn't gone straight through the goalkeeper's body! In 1971/72 Lee topped the First Division scoring charts with thirty-three goals, including fifteen from the penalty-spot. For this achievement he was awarded the bronze boot in the Golden Boot competition. In August 1974 he left City to join Derby County and in his first season at the Baseball Ground he helped the Rams win the League Championship. He retired in 1976. By then, the paper business which he had started while still with his first club Bolton was a great success and eventually secured him millionaire status. Lee also owned and trained racehorses, but in February 1994 he returned to Maine Road, heading a consortium that took control of the Manchester club. He resigned during the 1997/98 season but he remains on the board.

ANDY LOCHHEAD

Centre-Forward
Born 9.3.41, Lenzie

LEAGUE RECORD

	A	G
Burnley	225 (1)	101
Leicester City	40 (4)	12
Aston Villa	127 (4)	34
Oldham Athletic	44 (1)	10

HONOURS
Third Division Championship
1971/72 and 1973/74

ANDY LOCHHEAD was one of many fine young talents unearthed by Burnley's Glasgow-based scout Jimmy Stein, though Sunderland, who had invited him for a trial at Roker Park, passed up the opportunity to secure his signature.

After helping the Clarets' reserve side win the Central League Championship, Lochhead established himself as the club's first-choice for the no. 9 shirt and ended his first season, 1962/63, as the leading scorer with nineteen goals. He repeated this achievement the following season, by which time he had been joined in attack by Willie Irvine. The Scot and the Irishman were to form a formidable and effective goalscoring partnership during a time of change at Turf Moor in the mid-1960s. Lochhead is one of four Burnley players to have hit five goals in a first-team match – but he is the only Claret to do it twice! The first occasion was in April 1965 as Burnley beat Chelsea 6–2 and the second in the following January in a 7–0 demolition of Bournemouth in an FA Cup replay. During his time at Turf Moor, Lochhead also scored three hat-tricks and netted four goals on two occasions.

FACT

David Nish became the youngest FA Cup Final captain when he skippered Leicester City in 1969. He was 21 years and 7 months old.

In October 1968 Lochhead was transferred to Leicester City where he lined up alongside another newcomer, Allan Clarke. The two of them helped the Foxes to reach the FA Cup Final where they were beaten by Manchester City. However, the club's run to Wembley had been at the expense of their top-flight status and in February 1970 Lochhead was allowed to leave for Aston Villa. He was to suffer relegation again as Villa dropped into the Third Division for the first time in their history.

In 1971 he won a League Cup finalists' medal as Villa lost to Tottenham Hotspur at Wembley. A year later he was the club's leading scorer as Villa won the Third Division Championship in style. Lochhead joined Oldham Athletic in the summer of 1973 and at the end of his first season at Boundary Park won another Third Division Championship medal.

After a short spell in the NASL with Denver, he returned to Oldham as the club's player-coach before hanging up his boots in 1975, although he remained on the Latics' coaching staff. He left Oldham in 1979 and had a spell as manager of Padiham before returning to live and work in the Burnley area. For many years he has been involved in the licensing trade and after running a pub is now a steward at the Ighton Mount Bowling Club.

PETER LORIMER
Forward
Born 14.12.46, Dundee

LEAGUE RECORD

	A	G
Leeds United	504 (22)	168
York City	29	8

HONOURS
League Cup 1967/68
League Championship 1968/69
  and 1973/74
FA Cup 1971/72
Inter Cities Fairs Cup 1967/68
  and 1970/71
21 Scotland Caps

PETER LORIMER boasted one of the hardest shots in football,. He was Leeds United's youngest debutant, making his Football League debut in a 1–1 draw against Southampton in September 1962 when aged just 15 years and 289 days.

Lorimer once scored 176 goals in a season during his time at Stobswell School, Dundee, and had attracted the attention of a host of top clubs. Indeed, Leeds' manager Don Revie was in such a hurry to sign

him that he was stopped for speeding on his way up north! Lorimer joined the Yorkshire club in May 1962 and won Scottish Amateur caps on a tour of Kenya before turning professional in December 1963. In his early days at Elland Road he broke his leg but recovered to establish himself as an important member of the Leeds side. It was 1965/66 before he won back his regular place, helping Leeds to finish as runners-up in the First Division – they would finish in that spot another four times in Lorimer's career there. He won a League Championship medal in 1968/69 and the following season won the first of twenty-one caps when he played against Austria in November 1969. In fact, Lorimer was a key figure in Scotland's 1974 World Cup campaign.

Lorimer's thunderous shooting helped Leeds reap a rich harvest of honours but 1972/73 was the only season when he headed the club's scoring charts, his total of fifteen League goals including a last day hat-trick in a 6–1 defeat of Arsenal. In March 1979 Lorimer left Leeds to play for Toronto Blizzard but six months later he returned to England to sparkle in York City's ranks. In March 1980 he returned to Canada as player-coach with Vancouver Whitecaps. In December 1983, at the age of thirty-seven, Lorimer rejoined Leeds United – where he was older than his manager Eddie Gray! He played in midfield and during his second spell with the club overhauled John Charles' League aggregate of 153 goals before moving to non-League Whitby Town in December 1985.

On leaving Whitby, Lorimer had a brief spell as player-coach in Israel with Hapoel Haifa before returning to Leeds as landlord of the Commercial Inn. He also appears on Radio Leeds and sometimes on Radio Five as a summariser.

DAVE MACKAY
Left-Half
Born 14.11.34, Edinburgh

LEAGUE RECORD

	A	G
Tottenham Hotspur	268	42
Derby County	122	5
Swindon Town	25 (1)	1

HONOURS
League Championship 1960/61
FA Cup 1960/61, 1961/62 and 1966/67
Second Division Championship 1968/69
European Cup Winners' Cup 1962/63
22 Scotland Caps

DAVE MACKAY served his footballing apprenticeship with the romantically named Newtongrange Stars before joining Hearts as a part-time professional in April 1952. He signed up for full-time after completing his National Service and helped Hearts win the Scottish League Cup the following year. Success with Hearts soon brought representative honours and after playing for Scotland Under-23s against England and for the Scottish League against the Football League, he made his full international debut against Spain in May 1957. Although he helped Hearts win the Scottish League the following year, it was not until June 1958, after he had been voted Scotland's 'Player of the Year', that he won his next full cap. Two more caps and a 1959 Scottish League Cup winners' medal had been added to his collection before his move to Tottenham Hotspur in March 1959.

> **FACT**
>
> On 12 April 1969 Derby County won 1–0 at Millwall to clinch the Division Two Championship. The Rams had intended to play in an all-white strip, only to discover that Millwall were planning to do the same. The Lions duly loaned the Rams their second strip of red shirts and black shorts.

Spurs' manager Bill Nicholson later described Mackay's signing as his best day's work ever. Of his favourite drinking partner Jimmy Greaves said: 'he was the perfect wing-half: iron hard, dynamic, creative, skilful and a natural leader of men'. Mackay was also one of the most colourful and charismatic characters the game has ever seen. Three FA Cup wins, a League Championship (including the coveted 'double' in 1961) and a European Cup Winners' Cup triumph in nine unforgettable years at White Hart Lane provide ample evidence of Mackay's greatness. In March 1960 he became the first Scotsman to represent the Football League and was runner-up to the legendary Stanley Matthews as Footballer of the Year in 1963, which was some consolation for missing out through injury on his club's sensational victory over Athletico Madrid.

A twice-fractured leg sidelined him for the best part of two years but the real tragedy was that by the time he had returned to full fitness the great Tottenham side of the early 1960s was no more. Taking over as skipper, Mackay led Spurs to victory in the 1967 FA Cup Final against Chelsea.

In 1968, when a young Brian Clough was looking for an on-field general to lead his promising Derby County out of the Second Division, it was to the 33-year-old

Spurs war-horse that he turned. Twelve months later the title was won and Mackay, now playing as a sweeper, was named 'Footballer of the Year' for 1969 alongside fellow veteran Tony Book of Manchester City. After helping Derby establish themselves in the top flight, he moved to Swindon Town as player-manager and later had eleven months in charge at Nottingham Forest. When his former Derby boss Brian Clough left the Baseball Ground, Mackay replaced him and steered Derby to the League Championship in 1974/75. He left in November 1976 and went to Walsall where he suffered the first unsuccessful spell of his career. He subsequently took up the post as manager of the Al Arabi Sporting Club of Kuwait. He spent nine very successful years coaching in the Near East with Al Arabi and the Alba Shabab club of Dubai before returning to the Football League as manager of Doncaster Rovers. He later took on the role of general manager at Birmingham City but was unable to get the Blues out of the Third Division and resigned. He then had a spell in Qatar before ending his involvement with the game.

PAUL MADELEY
Defender/Midfielder
Born 20.9.44, Beeston, Leeds

HONOURS
League Cup 1967/68
League Championship 1968/69 and
  1973/74
FA Cup 1971/72
UEFA Cup 1967/68 and 1970/71
24 England Caps

PAUL MADELEY played in every position except in goal in a seventeen-year career at Elland Road. An England Schoolboy international, he began working in an insurance broker's office and played Yorkshire League football with Farsley Celtic. After being asked for trials by the Elland Road club, Madeley turned professional in the summer of 1962. Originally he was groomed as the successor to England's World Cup hero Jack Charlton but Don Revie soon realised that Madeley was a very versatile performer and this led to him making his debut against Manchester City in January 1964. In fact, Madeley's versatility led to him playing in nine different outfield positions within the space of one season!

Ignored at Under-23 level, he played for the Football League but then turned down the chance to go to Mexico for the 1970 World Cup. Though he was originally omitted from the squad, he was called up when Leeds team-mate Paul Reaney broke a leg. Madeley felt he wouldn't make the final squad when it was slimmed down and opted not to go. Luckily Alf Ramsey bore no grudges and in 1971 Madeley won the first of twenty-four caps when he played against Northern Ireland. Cautioned only twice in over seven hundred first-team appearances for the Yorkshire club, he won almost every honour both domestic and European.

Madeley retired in 1980 and opened a sports shop in Leeds, as well as keeping an interest in the very successful family home decor business. In December 1987 he and his brothers sold their chain of twenty-six DIY stores for £27 million. Five years later the former Leeds United player successfully underwent an operation to remove a brain tumour and now works as a property consultant, still based in his native Yorkshire.

RODNEY MARSH

Inside-Forward
Born 11.10.44, Hatfield

LEAGUE RECORD

	A	G
Fulham	79	27
Queen's Park Rangers	211	106
Manchester City	116 (2)	36

HONOURS
Third Division Championship 1966/67
League Cup 1966/67
9 England Caps

RODNEY MARSH was the crown prince of football, a flamboyant and precocious talent who should have won more than the nine England caps he gained. He began his career with Fulham and scored a magnificent volleyed goal on his League debut as the Cottagers beat Aston Villa 1–0. His career was making rapid progress until he sustained a serious injury at Leicester in February 1965 which left him partially deaf. After losing form he was sold to Queen's Park Rangers for £15,000 and made his debut for the Loftus Road club in a 1–1 draw at Peterborough United in March 1966.

The following season Marsh was the club's leading scorer with forty-four League and Cup goals as Rangers won the Third Division Championship and the League Cup. Included in the total were hat-tricks in the wins over Middlesbrough (Home 4–0), Mansfield Town (Away 7–1) and Poole Town (Home 3–2) and four goals against Colchester United (Home 5–0). In Rangers' 3–2 victory over West Bromwich Albion in the League Cup Final at Wembley Marsh scored with a spectacular effort.

In 1967/68, when Rangers won promotion to the First Division as runners-up to Ipswich Town, Marsh again topped the club's scoring charts, despite missing the first half of the season through injury. Even though Rangers were relegated after just one season in the top flight, Marsh continued to play for them for a further three seasons in the Second Division, netting a hat-trick against Blackpool (Home 6–1) and four goals against Tranmere Rovers (Home 6–0) in 1969/70 and hat-tricks against Birmingham City (Home 5–2) and Bolton Wanderers (Home 4–0) in 1970/71.

FACT

In August 1966 Colchester United half-back Bobby Blackwood broke his jaw in a collision with Queen's Park Rangers striker Les Allen in a Division Three match. In the return game in December Blackwood broke his jaw again in another collision with Allen.

After a number of offers for his services, Marsh, who had scored 134 goals in 242 games for Rangers, joined Manchester City for £200,000 in March 1972. With Marsh in the side, City became a joy to watch as his imaginative play set up a host of chances for his team-mates. Though not a prolific scorer with City, he did manage one hat-trick in a 4–1 defeat of York City in the League Cup competition of 1973/74. That season he won another League Cup medal as City lost 2–1 to Wolves in the final.

Marsh next moved to the United States to join Tampa Bay Rowdies and later managed them before retiring from playing. He returned to Fulham briefly in September 1976 to team up with George Best but injury dogged his stay. He became general manager of Tampa Bay Rowdies for eleven years before touring the country with a soccer roadshow in conjunction with George Best in 1994. Nowadays, Marsh works in journalism and as a television and radio pundit.

JIMMY McILROY

Inside-Forward
Born 25.10.31, Drumbeg

LEAGUE RECORD

	A	G
Burnley	439	116
Stoke City	96 (2)	16
Oldham Athletic	35 (4)	1

HONOURS

League Championship 1959/60
Second Division Championship
  1962/63
55 Northern Ireland Caps

The magical Irishman JIMMY McILROY began his career with Glentoran, becoming a regular in the side during the 1949/50 season. One of his team-mates was Billy Bingham, another future international, who was then, like McIlroy, under scrutiny from the English talent scouts. In March 1950 Burnley manager Frank Hill crossed the water to assess McIlroy's ability – the latest in a long line of admirers to do so – and after a particularly inspiring performance against Distillery McIlroy was on his way to Turf Moor.

McIlroy made his Burnley debut at Sunderland four days before his nineteenth birthday and within a year, while still a teenager, he won his first international cap against Scotland in Belfast. After beginning his Burnley career at inside-left, he switched to the right, his partnership with Jimmy Adamson knitting the team together. In August 1955 McIlroy was acknowledged as one of the finest football talents when he was chosen for Great Britain to play the Rest of Europe at Windsor Park in Belfast to commemorate the 75th anniversary of the Irish FA. When Burnley won the League Championship in 1959/60 and again in the two campaigns that followed, the McIlroy-Adamson partnership was at its best. In 1961/62 the Clarets came close to a League and Cup 'double', an inexplicable loss of form over the last few weeks of the season costing them dear. Jimmy McIlroy was just edged into second place in the poll for 'Footballer of the Year' by his captain Jimmy Adamson.

In February 1963 the unbelievable happened: McIlroy left Turf Moor to join Stoke City. He joined the likes of Dennis Viollet, Jackie Mudie and Stanley Matthews at the Victoria Ground and the Potters went on to win the Second Division Championship at the end of the season. They also reached their first major final in 1964 with McIlroy in the side, beaten 4–3 on aggregate by Leicester City in the two-legged League Cup Final.

In January 1966 McIlroy was recruited by Oldham Athletic as the Third Division club's player-manager. In August 1968 he returned to Stoke as chief coach but resigned a year later. He was out of the game until the summer of 1970 when, after a spell as Bolton's chief coach, he replaced Nat Lofthouse as manager. He spent just eighteen days in charge before leaving Burnden Park!

McIlroy then spent many years as a much respected journalist, initially with the *Lancashire Evening Telegraph*. He then joined the *Burnley Express* as a sports reporter and later developed a reputation as a fine feature writer. Now retired and living in the town where he will forever be a sporting hero, the popular Irishman spends his spare time playing golf.

FRANK McLINTOCK

Central Defender
Born 28.12.39, Glasgow

LEAGUE RECORD

	A	G
Leicester City	168	25
Arsenal	312 (2)	26
Queen's Park Rangers	126 (1)	5

HONOURS
League Championship 1970/71
FA Cup 1970/71
Inter Cities Fairs Cup 1969/70
9 Scotland Caps

FRANK McLINTOCK possessed the rare combination of toughness and elegance and soon became an important member of Leicester City's side. Oozing footballing class, it came as no surprise when he graduated to full Scottish honours or when Billy Wright's Arsenal eventually paid the Foxes their then record outgoing fee of £80,000 for his services. While at Filbert Street McLintock had played in two FA Cup Finals in 1961 and 1963, and both times was on the losing side.

During his first three seasons at Highbury Frank McLintock was probably the most consistent of all the Arsenal players, in a side that was probably the poorest for many years. In 1967/68 he became team captain and guided Arsenal to the League Cup Final against Leeds. In 1968/69 Arsenal finished fourth in the League, the club's highest position for fifteen seasons, and McLintock played in the League Cup Final against Swindon Town. At the beginning of the following season he asked for a transfer owing to the lack of success at Highbury. Fortunately for both him and the club he was persuaded to stay. In that season Arsenal gained their first major honour for seventeen years, winning the Inter Cities Fairs Cup. In 1970/71 McLintock became only the second player that century to captain a 'double'-winning side (Danny Blanchflower at Spurs in 1960/61 being the other) and was voted 'Footballer of the Year'. In 1971/72 he captained Arsenal to the FA Cup Final against Leeds, returning to Wembley for his sixth major final. In 1972/73 he led Arsenal to the runners-up spot in the First Division but at the end of that campaign he was surprisingly allowed to leave Highbury to join Queen's Park Rangers for £20,000.

It looked a certain case of the Scottish wing-half being written off too early as he assisted Rangers to a near-miss title bid in 1975/76. After four years at Loftus Road he entered management with Leicester City but was handed too much backroom responsibility too soon. Too many of his dealings in the transfer market bore the stamp of desperation and the Foxes were already certainties for relegation when he resigned in April 1978. His reluctance to commit himself to living in Leicester and to leave behind his London business interests didn't help. He returned to the capital and became adviser on the dire soccer-themed movie *Yesterday's Hero* before becoming youth coach at Queen's Park Rangers. He later managed Brentford and was assistant-manager at Millwall before working as a part-time players' agent. He then set up the 'Cash Converter' chain of shops and is now a regular commentator on Capital Gold Radio.

BOBBY MONCUR
Centre-Half
Born 19.1.45, Perth

LEAGUE RECORD

	A	G
Newcastle United	293 (3)	3
Sunderland	86	2
Carlisle United	11	0

HONOURS
Second Division Championship 1964/65
    and 1975/76
Inter Cities Fairs Cup 1968/69
16 Scotland Caps

BOBBY MONCUR was one of Newcastle United's finest captains and a superb central defender. A centre-back with the ability to read the game well and an aggressive, strong tackler, he was commanding in the air and a great marshal of the side. But he will always be remembered primarily for the hat-trick of goals he netted in the Inter Cities Fairs Cup Final of 1969 against Ujpesti Dosza.

Captain of the Scottish Schoolboys and a Youth international, Moncur was soon being tipped for the professional game. A number of top clubs showed an interest but Moncur opted for the Magpies. He played in various positions during his early days, with his first taste of success coming in the FA Youth Cup of 1962 when he scored United's winner in the final against Wolves.

Moncur played a handful of games during Newcastle's Second Division Championship winning season of 1964/65 but was something of a slow developer and manager Joe Harvey almost sold him to Norwich City! The deal fell through and Moncur worked hard at his game, gradually establishing himself in the no. 6 shirt. The 1967/68 season was the turning point in his career as he formed a fine central defensive partnership with John McNamee. Appointed club captain in place of Jim Iley, Moncur won full international honours for Scotland in May 1968 when he played against Holland in Amsterdam. After only six appearances for his country he was given the captaincy ahead of John Greig, going on to play in sixteen internationals.

In 1974 he led Newcastle United to the FA Cup Final at Wembley but the Magpies were outplayed by Liverpool, who ran out the winners 3–0. Following that FA Cup Final Moncur never kicked a ball for the club again. He was released by United, too soon thought many, though he had started to lack pace in the back four.

After 346 games for the Magpies, Moncur joined Sunderland and in 1975/76 helped the Wearsiders win the Second Division Championship. In November 1976 he joined Carlisle United as player-manager but resigned after the Cumbrian club slipped into Division Three. He then moved back to Edinburgh to take control of Heart of Midlothian, leading the Tynecastle side to the Scottish First Division Championship. Shortly afterwards he was appointed manager of

Plymouth Argyle but he left Home Park after a difference of opinion with the directors, and then quit football altogether.

Concentrating on business out of the game, he opened a sports shop in Gateshead. He also sailed a great deal, completing the Round Britain Yacht Race inside thirty-five days, as well as the Fastnet race and two Atlantic crossings. He returned to football as coach with Whitley Bay before being tempted into the Football League management scene with struggling Hartlepool. After leaving the game for the second time he opened a squash club. Moncur now runs his own yacht charter business in Newcastle.

LEAGUE RECORD

	A	G
Sunderland	537	0
Southampton	5	0
Birmingham City	66	0

HONOURS
FA Cup 1972/73

JIM MONTGOMERY
Goalkeeper
Born 9.10.43, Sunderland

JIM MONTGOMERY was one of the best goalkeepers in the Football League during the 1960s and might well have added a full England cap to his youth and Under-23 honours but for the presence of Gordon Banks. The Sunderland-born keeper joined his home-town club on leaving school in 1958 and turned professional at Roker Park in October 1960. He made his League debut for the Wearsiders in a 2–1 home win over Derby County in February 1962 and went on to become a permanent fixture for the next fourteen seasons, though he missed much of the 1964/65 season with a hand injury. He was ever-present for Sunderland in five seasons including 1963/64 when the club won promotion to the First Division as runners-up to Leeds United.

Montgomery won an FA Cup winners' medal in 1973 when Second Division Sunderland completely ripped up the form book to pull off one of the biggest upsets in a Wembley final by beating Leeds United 1–0. Yet the game is often remembered for the save by Jim Montgomery that enabled the Wearsiders to hang on to the Cup rather than for the goal that won it! Midway through the second half Leeds United's Trevor Cherry linked up with his attacking forwards and put in a diving header which Montgomery did well to parry. The ball ran loose to Peter Lorimer who hit the ball hard and true from close range, only for Montgomery to twist in the air and fling out his arms to tip the ball on to the underside of the crossbar for a truly amazing double save. Montgomery's superb effort sapped Leeds' spirit and although they pushed forward, somewhat belatedly, anything less than victory would have been hard on underdogs Sunderland.

Montgomery went on to appear in a club record total of 623 League and Cup games for the Wearsiders. Following a loan spell with Southampton, he joined Birmingham City on a free transfer. After two seasons at St Andrew's, he joined Nottingham Forest as cover for Peter Shilton. Montgomery returned to Birmingham as temporary coach for a short time and then went home to Sunderland to become senior coach at Roker Park. He was thirty-seven when the Rokerites re-signed him as a non-contract reserve goalkeeper. Formerly a director of youth football at Roker Park, Jim Montgomery is now goalkeeping coach at Darlington.

BOBBY MOORE

Central Defender
Born 12.4.41, Barking
Died 24.2.93

LEAGUE RECORD

	A	G
West Ham United	543 (1)	24
Fulham	124	1

HONOURS
FA Cup 1963/64
European Cup Winners' Cup
  1964/65
108 England Caps

BOBBY MOORE was the greatest West Ham player of all time, and the first captain to lift three trophies at Wembley Stadium in three consecutive years: the FA Cup in 1964, the European Cup Winners' Cup in 1965 (both with the Hammers) and the World Cup in 1966. Moore's development was steady. He played a record eighteen times for England Youth, turned professional in June 1958 and followed the conventional route towards the international team with eight Under-23 caps and an international debut in Peru in May 1962. As a twenty-year-old international, his earning potential – both inside and outside the game – was considerable. When he was made England's youngest-ever captain for the match against Czechoslovakia in May 1963, that potential became enormous.

'Homely' was the adjective most frequently used to describe West Ham in those days but then the friendly club became very successful. They won the 1964 FA Cup Final, beating Preston North End 3–2, and Moore was elected 'Footballer of the Year'. Cup victory sent West Ham into Europe. The team just kept on getting better and on a warm spring evening at Wembley they produced what many people still regard as the finest performance by a British side in Europe, beating TSV Munich 1860 to win the European Cup Winners' Cup. Moore's leadership of West Ham had established his status as one of the most influential people in the British game. He was now in the front rank of international defenders, his natural ability refined by Greenwood and England manager Alf Ramsey and his temperament honed by seasons of world-class competition.

In the 1966 World Cup Moore won the Player of Players Award at the end of the tournament, and such was the calibre of his performance that even in a competition featuring all the world's finest players there was no conceivable alternative. Moore actually became a better player in the seasons after the 1966 triumph. West Ham started to fall on hard times but Moore's own game was completely unaffected. In 1973, after appearing in 642 games for the Hammers, he joined Fulham and played against West Ham in the FA Cup Final of 1975. After

FACT

West Ham United scored three goals in each round of the FA Cup in 1963/64, including the Final. They were also involved in one replay after a 1–1 draw.

breaking Bobby Charlton's England appearance record, he played only one more game for his country.

Sadly, after leaving Craven Cottage Moore was not able to repeat his on-field success and after coaching and managing in Denmark and Hong Kong he took charge of Southend United. The Shrimps were relegated to Division Four in 1984 and then struggled near the foot of the League's basement before Moore resigned in April 1986. He then decided to concentrate on journalism and broadcasting but in February 1993 he announced that he was suffering from cancer. He died just a few days later.

WILLIE MORGAN

Winger
Born 2.10.44, Glasgow

LEAGUE RECORD

	A	G
Burnley	195 (1)	19
Manchester United	236 (2)	25
Bolton Wanderers	154 (1)	10
Blackpool	41 (1)	4

HONOURS

Second Division Championship
  1974/75 and 1978/79
21 Scotland Caps

One of the finest post-war wingers in British football, WILLIE MORGAN began his career with Burnley. Brilliant on the ball and able to shake off opponents at will, Morgan quickly became one of the most feared wingers in the game. His crosses were delivered with pinpoint accuracy and he supplied them regularly to Willie Irvine and Andy Lochhead during the 1965/66 season. The pair scored sixty goals between them in League and Cup, steering the Clarets to third in Division One and a place in Europe. His performances inevitably had the big city clubs watching and it became only a matter of time before he left Turf Moor. In the summer of 1968 European Champions Manchester United moved in with an offer of £117,000 – too much for the Clarets to refuse, especially with David Thomas waiting in the wings.

Morgan made his United debut against Tottenham Hotspur on the right wing. On the other wing was an up-and-coming youngster called George Best! Morgan's first goals for the Reds came in an 8–1 destruction of Queen's Park Rangers at Old Trafford in March 1969, when he scored a hat-trick. There were to be a few lean years ahead for the Old Trafford club, certainly in the League, although Willie Morgan enjoyed some stirring campaigns in the various cup competitions. As holders, United reached the semi-final of the European Cup in 1969, while the following year they faced defeat in the semi-finals of both the FA and League Cup. There was another League Cup semi-final defeat in 1971.

In 1974, following United's relegation to Division Two, Morgan was off to West Germany as a member of Scotland's World Cup party, playing the last of his twenty-one internationals against Yugoslavia in Frankfurt. In 1974/75 United won the Second Division Championship, Morgan winning the first club honour of his career at the age of thirty. However, following the emergence of Steve Coppell, Morgan found himself surplus to requirements at Old Trafford and rejoined Burnley. The move was not a success and in March 1976 he moved to Bolton Wanderers. He was instrumental in the Whites winning the Second Division Championship and reaching the League Cup semi-final. While at Bolton he enjoyed summer loan periods in the NASL but in September 1980 he moved to Blackpool where he ended his first-class career.

Morgan, who invested his money in a chain of launderettes, briefly opened a sports shop in Altrincham but now the former winger lives comfortably in Cheshire, helping to run a successful marketing and promotions company in Manchester.

LEAGUE RECORD

	A	G
Liverpool	36	6
Everton	257 (2)	43
Oldham Athletic	6	1

HONOURS

League Championship 1962/63 and 1969/70

JOHNNY MORRISSEY
Winger
Born 18.4.40, Liverpool

JOHNNY MORRISSEY began his career with Liverpool but in September 1962 he moved across Stanley Park to Goodison for a fee of £10,000. The transfer had been sanctioned by the Liverpool board but without the agreement of manager Bill Shankly, who made it quite clear that any further transactions without his blessing would result in his departure from Anfield! Morrissey's early displays for the Blues certainly seemed to strengthen Shankly's case, for after coming close on a number of occasions the Everton winger opened his account in the Merseyside derby as the Blues drew 2–2 against their arch rivals. The following week Morrissey netted a hat-trick in a 4–2 home win over West Bromwich Albion, going on to help Everton win the League Championship in his first season with the club.

Despite this success Morrissey found that he had to share the no. 1 shirt with Derek Temple and indeed he missed out on FA Cup glory in 1966 when the Blues beat Sheffield Wednesday 3–2. Determined to claim a regular first-team spot, Morrissey hit the best form of his career as the decade came to a close. He was the man who guaranteed Everton a place in the 1968 FA Cup Final with a dramatic penalty winner against high-flying Leeds United in the semi-final at Old Trafford. The tenacious and gutsy winger placed the spot-kick wide of Welsh international keeper Gary Sprake to set up a Wembley showdown with West Bromwich Albion, a match the Blues lost 1–0.

Morrissey's ball control with either foot was impeccable while his intelligent assessment of attacking situations proved the downfall of many of Everton's opponents. He was at his most effective when collecting from deep positions. Hugging the touchline, he was explosively quick over very short distances and, although he occasionally cut inside to hit a powerful shot with his right foot, he was at his best when tricking his way to the by-line and floating over one of his devastatingly accurate crosses.

Morrissey was the 'Pocket Hercules' of a side which won national acclaim for their cultured football in 1969/70, winning their second League Championship. Two seasons later Morrissey found it difficult to hold down a regular first-team place and left to join Oldham Athletic. Sadly, it wasn't too long before injury ended his career at Boundary Park.

Now a highly successful businessman on Merseyside, Johnny Morrissey was one of the shrewdest buys the Blues have ever made.

ALAN MULLERY

Wing-Half
Born 23.11.41, Notting Hill

LEAGUE RECORD

	A	G
Fulham	363 (1)	37
Tottenham Hotspur	312	25

HONOURS
FA Cup 1966/67
League Cup 1970/71
UEFA Cup 1971/72
35 England Caps

Within two months of signing for Fulham as a seventeen-year-old professional, wing-half ALAN MULLERY had made his League debut in a 5–2 home win over Leyton Orient in February 1959. He kept his place in the side alongside stars like Johnny Haynes, Graham Leggatt and Tosh Chamberlain, and at the end of the season Fulham won promotion to the First Division. A permanent fixture in the Cottagers' team, his impressive performances in the top flight led to him winning the first of three England Under-23 caps when he played against Italy in November 1960. He had played in 218 League and Cup games for Fulham when in March 1964 Spurs paid £72,500 for his services.

Two months later Mullery played for the Football League against the Italian League and after one more outing with the Football League he won his first full cap against Holland in December 1964. Kept out of the England team by the brilliance of Nobby Stiles, he did not win his second cap until May 1967, four days after winning an FA Cup winners' medal against Chelsea. After that he became an England regular, winning thirty-three more caps.

In 1968 he became club captain and led Spurs to victory in the 1971 League Cup Final. However, in October of that year he began to suffer from a serious pelvic strain which put him out of action for six months. When he had recovered he went on loan to Fulham but after a month was recalled owing to a lengthy injury list at White Hart Lane. Leading the club into their UEFA Cup semi-final with AC Milan, he clinched the tie with a brilliant 20-yard volley at the San Siro Stadium before going on to secure the trophy with a header – he knocked himself out in the process – in the second leg of the final against Wolves. He returned to Craven Cottage in the summer of 1972 for a fee of £65,000 after appearing in 429 games for Spurs. In 1975 he won an FA Cup runners-up medal after Fulham had been beaten 2–0 by West Ham United. Mullery, who had been made skipper by manager Alec Stock, was elected 'Footballer of the Year' and awarded the MBE.

FACT

Though the risk of serious injury is an ever-present threat, and all professional players expect to miss games through injury at some point in their careers, not every injury is sustained on the pitch. In 1964 Alan Mullery missed a tour of Brazil after he ricked his back cleaning.

On leaving the game, he entered management with Brighton, leading them from the Third to the First Division before moving to Charlton. He spent only a year with the Addicks before managing Crystal Palace and Queen's Park Rangers for two years each and then ending his involvement with the game with another spell at Brighton. Since then he has worked as a football presenter on London's Capital Gold Radio station.

KEITH NEWTON

Full-Back
Born 23.6.41, Manchester
Died 16.6.98

LEAGUE RECORD

	A	G
Blackburn Rovers	306	9
Everton	48 (1)	1
Burnley	209	5

HONOURS
League Championship 1969/70
Second Division Championship
 1972/73
27 England Caps

Brought up in Manchester, KEITH NEWTON played his early football as an inside-forward and was spotted by the Blackburn Rovers' scouting system, arriving at Ewood Park in 1958. He was a member of the Rovers' team which won the FA Youth Cup in 1959, playing alongside internationals of the future like Mike England and Fred Pickering. It was at left-back that he established a regular place in the Blackburn side, his smooth cultured style, speed and effectiveness in the tackle ensuring he would be an important member of the Rovers' defence for many years to come. At the start of the 1964/65 season he switched to right-back, the position in which he won the first of his four England Under-23 caps. However, his full international debut came at left-back in a Wembley rehearsal against West Germany in February 1966, England winning 1–0. Newton missed out on the World Cup that summer but, despite Rovers now being in the Second Division, he became a regular in the England side, operating in both full-back positions, alternating with George Cohen and Ray Wilson.

In December 1969 Newton joined Everton and played his part in bringing the League Championship to Goodison Park in his first season, although he missed the run-in with injury. That summer he was off to Mexico with England's World Cup squad, but his international career was to end there after the epic quarter-final defeat by West Germany.

Over the next couple of seasons he found himself in and out of the Everton side and in May 1972 he joined Burnley on a free transfer. In his first season at Turf Moor he was one of six ever-present players as the Clarets swept to the Second Division title. He missed very few matches during his Burnley career. The years finally caught up with him, and with the Turf Moor club back in the Second Division he made the last of his 564 League appearances at Brighton in February 1978. Released in the summer, he played non-League football for Morecambe and Clitheroe, where he was the club's player-manager. After hanging up his boots, he set up a sports trophy business and then a newsagent's in Blackburn before going to work with a local garage group in the same East Lancashire town. Keith Newton passed away in the summer of 1998.

LEAGUE RECORD

	A	G
Manchester City	561 (3)	26
Chester City	211	15
Port Vale	1	0

HONOURS
Second Division Championship 1965/66
League Championship 1967/68
FA Cup 1968/69
League Cup 1969/70 and 1975/76
European Cup Winners' Cup 1969/70

ALAN OAKES
Midfielder
Born 7.9.42, Winsford

ALAN OAKES played the first of his 669 games for Manchester City – more than any other player – on 14 November 1959 against Chelsea, as a stand-in for the injured Ken Barnes. In his debut season he had to help City fight against relegation, which was only avoided in the penultimate game of the campaign, when Colin Barlow's goal secured victory over Preston North End. It was towards the end of the following season that Ken Barnes retired from the first-class game and Oakes was in! His early years at Maine Road in the first half of the 1960s were spent in a poor City side. However, he held on and was rewarded with plenty of honours in the remainder of his career with the Manchester City. He won a Second Division Championship medal, followed by a League Championship medal, two League Cup winners' medals, an FA Cup winners' medal and a European Cup Winners' Cup medal.

Oakes didn't manage to acquire a full England cap but he did play for the Football League against the Scottish League at Hampden Park in March 1969. Over the two seasons prior to this, he had been selected for the full England squad on three occasions but still awaited that elusive first cap. There have certainly been more flamboyant footballers than Alan Oakes who have won an England cap, but they were probably not as talented. He was a player who made great surging runs from midfield, Young and Coleman in particular benefiting from his attacking play.

Despite playing at wing-half, he was fortunate enough to score a number of goals for City. Against Athletico Bilbao in the second leg of the European Cup Winners' Cup match at Maine Road, after the first leg had been drawn 3–3, he let fly from fully 30 yards as the Spanish defence backed off and the ball rocketed into the net. When Swindon Town were the opponents, and Mike Summerbee, not yet with City, threw the ball to a surprised Oakes, he killed it, swung round and hit it terrifically hard from 40 yards with his left foot to score!

Alan Oakes was rewarded with a testimonial against Manchester United in 1972 but four years later, having helped City to yet another success at Wembley, he signed for Chester, later becoming the club's player-manager. When he lost his job he joined Port Vale as coach but in October 1983, during an injury crisis at the club, he actually played in the match against Plymouth Argyle – at the age of forty-one! Demoted to youth team coach he decided to quit the club and later returned to the Cestrians as coach. Now his son keeps goal for Wolverhampton Wanderers, but Oakes has no involvement with the game.

JOHN O'HARE

Forward
Born 24.9.46, Dumbarton

LEAGUE RECORD

	A	G
Sunderland	51	14
Derby County	247 (1)	65
Leeds United	6	1
Nottingham Forest	94 (7)	14

HONOURS
Second Division Championship
  1968/69
League Championship 1971/72 and
  1977/78
League Cup 1977/78
European Cup 1979/80
13 Scotland Caps

JOHN O'HARE played his early football for Drumchapel Amateurs before signing amateur forms for Sunderland in 1962. He turned professional in October 1963 and was helped by Brian Clough who was Sunderland's youth coach. O'Hare was Clough's first signing for Derby County in August 1967, the striker costing the Rams £22,000. In his second season at the Baseball Ground, O'Hare, who netted ten goals in forty-one games, helped Derby win the Second Division Championship. During the course of that 1968/69 season he was chosen to represent Scotland at Under-23 level for the match against England but the game was cancelled because of bad weather. But he finally made it in January 1970 when he played for the Scottish Under-23s against Wales Under-23s and scored two goals in a 4–0 victory.

The following season O'Hare made such a great impression that he played in all three of the Home Internationals for the full Scotland team in April 1970 and remained in the side for the next couple of seasons, winning thirteen caps. His first goal for his country was the only goal of the game against Denmark in the European Nations Cup game in November 1970.

O'Hare was Derby County's leading scorer on a number of occasions and won a League Championship medal in 1971/72. But after seven years at the Baseball Ground he joined Leeds United in a deal involving John McGovern. Under the brief but turbulent reign of Brian Clough, O'Hare played in just six games for Leeds before following Clough to Nottingham Forest with McGovern in February 1975. That move opened up another chapter of glory as O'Hare won another League Championship medal in 1977/78, along with a League Cup winners' medal, and a European Cup winners' medal in 1980.

He was loaned to Dallas Tornado in the NASL in 1977 and left the professional game in the summer of 1981. He was later with Belper Town, Derby Carriage & Wagon FC and Ockbrook FC and became manager of Central Midlands League side Stanton in March 1988. After leaving full-time football, he ran a pub near Derby, worked for International Combustion and then as a stock controller at Toyota's European plant on the outskirts of Derby.

TERRY PAINE
Winger
Born 23.3.39, Winchester

LEAGUE RECORD

	A	G
Southampton	709 (4)	160
Hereford United	106 (5)	8

HONOURS
Third Division Championship 1959/60
19 England Caps

TERRY PAINE began his football career with his home-town club Winchester, then managed by Harry Osman, a former Southampton forward. Osman recommended young Paine to Saints' manager Ted Bates and in August 1956 he was added to the club's playing staff. He made his Southampton debut as a seventeen-year-old in a 3–3 home draw against Brentford in March 1957. Alternating from left to right wing, he was ever-present in 1958/59 and again in 1959/60 when the club won the Third Division Championship. That season Paine was irrepressible and was rewarded with his first England Under-23 cap when he played against Holland. In 1960/61, the club's first season back in the Second Division, Paine scored twenty-five League and Cup goals. On 18 November 1961 he missed the home match against Sunderland after appearing in 160 consecutive League games from 22 March 1958, but was ever-present again in 1962/63.

In 1963 Paine won the first of nineteen full international caps for England when he played against Czechoslovakia, and later that year scored a hat-trick at Wembley in an 8–3 win over Northern Ireland to become the first outside-right to score three goals for England since Stanley Matthews in 1937. He was part of Alf Ramsey's plans for the 1966 World Cup, though he only played in the 2–0 win over Mexico, a match in which he was injured. It was Paine's last international appearance, all of his caps being won when he was a Second Division player.

FACT

There have been few other League matches in the post-war era quite like the one on 18 September 1965, in the matter of a team gaining an overwhelming victory despite losing a first-minute goal. In a home Division One match against Wolverhampton Wanderers, Southampton were one down after thirty-five seconds, yet they won 9–3.

In 1963/64 Paine finished the season as the Saints' joint leading scorer with twenty-one League goals, including hat-tricks in wins over Rotherham United (Away 3–2) and Derby County (Home 6–4). He was an important member of the Southampton side that won promotion to the First Division in 1965/66 and the following season his endless stream of pin-point crosses brought Ron Davies thirty-seven goals in forty-one League games. The following season saw Paine used in more of a midfield role and there were even calls for him to be reinstated in the England side as his passing skills began to unlock even the tightest of First Division defences. Staying free from injury, Paine broke both the club appearance and goalscoring records, playing in 801 League and Cup games and scoring 183 goals.

In 1974 he left the Dell to join Hereford United, playing in another 106 games and so appearing in more League games than any other player. When he hung up his boots, he went into management with Cheltenham Town. Awarded the MBE for his services to football, he was proprietor of a café and a greengrocery business and also a Cheltenham licensee before emigrating to South Africa where he now works as a football coach.

MARTIN PETERS
Midfielder
Born 8.11.43, Plaistow

LEAGUE RECORD

	A	G
West Ham United	302	81
Tottenham Hotspur	189	46
Norwich City	206 (1)	44
Sheffield United	23 (1)	4

HONOURS
League Cup 1970/71 and 1972/73
European Cup Winners' Cup 1964/65
UEFA Cup 1971/72
67 England Caps

MARTIN PETERS was described as 'ten years ahead of his time' by England manager Sir Alf Ramsey in 1966, and he was probably the least famous of the three West Ham players who did so much to help their country win the World Cup. An England Schoolboy, he won England Youth honours after signing apprentice forms for the Hammers. He played five times for England Under-23s and sixty-seven times for the full national side.

Peters made his West Ham debut in a 4–1 win over Cardiff City on Good Friday 1962 and went on to appear in every position for the club including goalkeeper. A member of West Ham's European Cup Winners' Cup team of 1965 and the League Cup Final team of 1966, he played in 364 games for the Hammers, scoring exactly a hundred goals, including a hat-trick in a 4–0 win over West Bromwich Albion in August 1968.

An elegant, goalscoring midfield player with first-class technical skills and a high work-rate, he left Upton Park for Spurs in March 1970 for a British record fee of £200,000, with Jimmy Greaves going to West Ham in part exchange. Peters won his first representative honour as a Spurs player, as a substitute for the Football League against the Scottish League, within days of putting pen to paper. A member of the Spurs teams that won the League Cup in 1971 and 1973

FACT

In 1963/64 West Ham United might have been tempted to change their nickname to the 'B's as they had twelve players whose surnames began with this letter: Jim Barratt, Peter Bennett, David Bickles, John Bond, Eddie Bovington, Ronnie Boyce, Peter Brabrook, Martin Britt, Ken Brown, Jack Burkett, Dennis Burnett and Johnny Byrne.

and the UEFA Cup in 1972, he also played in the UEFA Cup Final of 1974. He made 278 League and Cup appearances for Spurs, scoring eighty-seven goals, but in March 1975 he was allowed to leave White Hart Lane and joined Norwich City for £50,000. He made almost a hundred consecutive appearances from his debut for the Canaries and was twice voted the club's 'Player of the Year' before being appointed player-manager of Sheffield United.

At Bramall Lane he took his total of Football League appearances past the seven hundred mark. He retired from football after his dismissal by the Blades but, like so many before him, he was unable to translate his success on the field

into management. He subsequently returned to the playing side of the game with Gorleston Town. Awarded the MBE in the 1978 New Year's Honours List, Peters later worked for a fruit-machine firm before linking up with his former Hammers and England team-mate Geoff Hurst at a motor repair insurance company. Today he is still involved in football through promotional work for Tottenham Hotspur.

LEAGUE RECORD

	A	G
Blackburn Rovers	134	61
Everton	97	56
Birmingham City	74	27
Blackpool	48 (1)	24

HONOURS
3 England Caps

FRED PICKERING
Centre-Forward
Born 19.1.41, Blackburn

One of the game's finest post-war strikers, FRED PICKERING began his career as a full-back with Blackburn Rovers. He had already tasted success in the Rovers' junior teams, helping to win the FA Youth Cup in 1959, but when he was given a first-team chance he failed to make a lasting impression.

Nevertheless, Blackburn manager Jack Marshall decided to gamble on him at centre-forward after some powerful displays in that position while playing with the reserves. Despite his initial clumsy approach work, Pickering had the happy knack of putting the ball in the net and was soon to make a name for himself. He had begun to add pace and power to his game and played havoc with the best defenders in the land. However, after fifty-nine goals in 123 League games, Pickering became unsettled and wanted a transfer. Blackburn were in their best League position for years but incredibly, and controversially, the club let him go. A fee of £85,000 took him to Everton. At the time, he was the highest priced player in a domestic transfer deal. It was to prove a wise signing for the Blues, as the tall, dashing centre-forward threatened defences throughout the First Division.

FACT
On 7 September 1968 Birmingham City's Geoff Vowden became the first substitute in the Football League to score a hat-trick. His three goals came in a 5–1 win over Huddersfield Town.

Pickering began well by scoring a hat-trick on his home debut as the Blues beat Nottingham Forest 6–1, yet it was in the final few games of that season that Everton lost the title – Pickering possibly upsetting the team's balance and rhythm. However, he still netted nine goals in nine matches.

Two months later Pickering scored another hat-trick in his first match for England as the United States were beaten 10–0. In 1964/65 he proved to be worth every penny of his huge transfer fee, collecting twenty-seven goals, including a hat-trick during a 4–1 home win over Tottenham Hotspur. Pickering remained in splendid form the following season but in March 1966 in the Merseyside derby he twisted awkwardly and his leg collapsed under him. After missing a couple of games he returned, only for the leg to go again against Sheffield United when he jumped for a high ball and came down on his knee. He had to miss both the FA Cup semi-final and the final against Sheffield Wednesday. Popular with the Everton fans, with fewer injuries and a different temperament he could have become one of the really great Everton footballers.

In August 1967 he moved to Birmingham City, proving to be a prolific marksman for the St Andrew's club. He returned to the north-west in 1969 to join Blackpool. After helping the Seasiders win promotion to the First Division he rejoined Blackburn Rovers in March 1971. Sadly he was released the following season after manager Ken Furphy claimed he was out of condition. He attempted to revive his career with Brighton and Hove Albion but without much success. He then returned to live and work in his home-town of Blackburn, where he became a forklift truck driver in a local factory.

RAY POINTER
Centre-Forward
Born 10.10.36, Cramlington

RAY POINTER was Burnley's most prolific scorer in post-war football and his non-stop efforts during every match endeared him to the fans at Turf Moor where he enjoyed cult status. During his first full season, 1958/59, Pointer was easily the Clarets' top scorer with twenty-seven goals – the club's best haul by an individual player for thirty years and only bettered since by Willie Irvine with twenty-nine in 1965/66. Pointer's exploits in front of goal were bound to catch the eye of the England selectors and in the summer of 1959 he took his place in the Under-23 side to take on Italy in the San Siro Stadium, scoring twice in a 3–0 win.

Burnley won the League Championship in 1959/60: Pointer scored twenty-three goals and played in every League and Cup game that season. The goals continued to flow from the head and the feet of the energetic Pointer and in September 1961 he was chosen to lead the attack for the full England side against Luxembourg at Highbury. He found the net in a 4–1 win and scored again in a 2–0 World Cup qualifier victory over Portugal, but it was to be the last of his full international appearances.

Pointer was Burnley's top scorer again in 1961/62 with twenty-five goals as the Clarets came within three games of clinching the League and Cup 'double'. In April 1963 Pointer chipped a bone in his ankle during the match at Nottingham Forest, an injury that signalled the beginning of the end of his illustrious Burnley career.

In August 1965 he moved to Bury, scoring seventeen goals in nineteen games but by Christmas he was on the move again, this time to ambitious Coventry City. With the Sky Blues well on their way to promotion to the top flight, Pointer joined Portsmouth in January 1967. He was a first-team regular at Fratton Park until he was well into his thirties but by then he was playing in midfield and combining his playing duties with coaching Pompey's youngsters.

On leaving Portsmouth he teamed up with former Burnley manager Harry Potts at Blackpool, Pointer becoming the Seasiders' youth coach. On leaving Bloomfield Road he worked for two years on the Fylde as well as playing and coaching in the local amateur leagues. There followed coaching posts with Burnley and Bury but in 1990, at the age of fifty-four, he decided to retire, ending his involvement with the game.

JOHN RITCHIE

Centre-Forward
Born 12.7.41, Kettering

LEAGUE RECORD

	A	G
Stoke City	261 (9)	135
Sheffield Wednesday	88 (1)	34

HONOURS
League Cup 1971/72

The most prolific goalscorer in Stoke City's history with 171 League and Cup goals, JOHN RITCHIE was signed from non-League Kettering for £2,500 on a scout's recommendations. Making his League debut against Cardiff City in April 1963, he went on to score fifty-nine goals in ninety-one appearances in his first two seasons at the Victoria Ground. He took a particular liking to Sheffield

Wednesday, hitting his first hat-trick against them in a 4–4 draw midway through the 1963/64 season. In the following campaign he scored all four goals in City's 4–1 defeat of the Owls.

In November 1966 Ritchie joined the Hillsborough club in a £70,000 deal. The Stoke supporters were absolutely amazed that such a proven goalscorer as Ritchie had been allowed to leave the Victoria Ground and there was unrest among the Potters' faithful for many weeks. Ritchie, who was Wednesday's most expensive signing, certainly began well enough at Hillsborough, netting a hat-trick in a 3–0 third-round FA Cup win over Queen's Park Rangers. In his first two seasons with the Owls he scored thirty-seven goals in seventy-seven games but at the outset of the 1968/69 season he began to suffer a spate of niggling injuries. In the close season he rejoined Stoke for a meagre £25,000 as Tony Waddington, to his credit, acknowledged the move to Hillsborough had been a grave mistake! During his time with Sheffield Wednesday Ritchie had been called into the Football League side and scored twice in a 7–2 win over the League of Ireland.

On his return to the Victoria Ground Ritchie teamed up with Jimmy Greenhoff. Leading the forward line with distinction, he helped Stoke reach the Football League Cup Final where they beat Chelsea 2–1. However, in the match against Ipswich Town at Portman Road on 24 September 1974 John Ritchie broke his leg. It was his last game for the club and apart from the occasional appearance for Stafford Rangers it ended his playing career. On the brighter side it enabled him to concentrate on his pottery business, selling crockery to hotels and restaurants from his base just a short distance from Stoke's previous home, the Victoria Ground.

LEAGUE RECORD

	A	G
Tottenham Hotspur	153 (4)	25
Arsenal	45 (1)	7
Ipswich Town	87	10
Stoke City	99 (15)	12
Walsall	16	0
Crewe Alexandra	32 (1)	0

HONOURS
FA Cup 1966/67
1 Scotland Cap

JIMMY ROBERTSON
Winger
Born 17.12.44, Glasgow

JIMMY ROBERTSON was a Middlesbrough junior and a part-timer with Celtic before joining Cowdenbeath. He played in the Cowdenbeath side as a sixteen-year-old amateur, represented Scotland at Youth level and won an amateur cap against Northern Ireland before joining St Mirren. Three months after winning his first Under-23 cap for Scotland against Wales, he was transferred to Tottenham Hotspur for £25,000.

A fast, well-balanced winger who loved to cut inside and try a shot on goal, Jimmy Robertson was able to play on either flank, but he is best remembered at White Hart Lane as a right-winger, a player who supplied the ammunition for the likes of Jimmy Greaves and Alan Gilzean. After his move to White Hart Lane Robertson won three more caps for Scotland at Under-23 level before winning his one and only cap at full international level against Wales in October 1964.

Blessed with great pace and an accurate crosser of the ball, Robertson also varied his play by cleverly holding up the ball and creating chances with perceptive passes through the defence. He was a popular player with the Tottenham faithful and his finest performance for the White Hart Lane club probably came in the 1967 FA Cup Final against Chelsea when he scored the opening goal to launch Spurs on the way to their fifth FA Cup victory.

With wingers seemingly drifting out of fashion, Robertson was allowed to leave White Hart Lane in October 1968, moving to rivals Arsenal in a £55,000 deal which saw David Jenkins travel in the opposite direction. It was not one of manager Bill Nicholson's better decisions as Robertson had plenty of good football left in him. Due mainly to the presence of George Armstrong, Jimmy Robertson never really settled at Highbury and it was no surprise that after less than two years he joined Ipswich Town. After useful service at Portman Road, he joined Stoke City before winding down his career with Walsall and Crewe Alexandra.

After settling in the Potteries, Robertson became director of the Task Force Group, a computer insurance company, but more often than not he is now to be found working and playing at Newcastle-under-Lyme Golf Club.

BRYAN 'POP' ROBSON

Forward
Born 11.11.45, Sunderland

LEAGUE RECORD

	A	G
Newcastle United	205 (1)	82
West Ham United	227	94
Sunderland	146 (8)	60
Carlisle United	69 (3)	26
Chelsea	11 (4)	3

HONOURS
Second Division Championship
1964/65, 1974/75 and 1979/80
Inter Cities Fairs Cup 1968/69

BRYAN ROBSON began his career with Newcastle United. Although he found the net on his Magpies' debut, it took the small, chunky forward several seasons to become a deadly goalscorer. In fact, at one time Robson was rated as the best uncapped striker in England. He was a fixture in Joe Harvey's side of the mid-1960s but it wasn't until he teamed up with Welsh international Wyn Davies in 1968/69 that he started to put the ball in the net with great regularity. He won a Second Division Championship medal and an Inter Cities Fairs Cup medal but after a war of words with Harvey he was transferred to West Ham United for a club record fee of £120,000 in February 1971.

As at Newcastle, he scored on his Hammers' debut in a 2–0 win over Nottingham Forest, and in 1972/73 he scored twenty-eight League goals (including a hat-trick in a 4–3 win over Southampton) to make him the League's joint top-scorer with Exeter City's Fred Binney. At the end of the 1973/74 season he returned to his native north-east to join Sunderland. An ever-present in his first season with his home-town club, scoring nineteen goals in forty-two games, he helped the Wearsiders win promotion to the First Division in 1974/75 as Second Division Champions but in October 1976 he returned to Upton Park to rejoin the Hammers. He continued to find the net with great regularity and in 1978/79 he topped the Second Division scoring charts with twenty-four goals, netting a hat-trick in a 3–0 home win over Millwall and winning the Adidas Golden Boot award. Although he was offered a new contract, he returned to play for Sunderland again in the summer of 1979.

Top-scoring with twenty goals, he won another Second Division Championship medal in 1979/80 but then joined Carlisle United for a couple of seasons. In August 1982 he moved to Chelsea. He was now thirty-six and, although his stay in the Chelsea first team seemed likely to be a short one, manager John Neal was confident that his professionalism would help transform the spirit at the club. Robson later returned to Roker Park for a third time as Sunderland's player-coach before being appointed manager of Carlisle United. He then relinquished the post to play for Gateshead in the Northern Premier League before later coaching at Manchester United.

Robson, who at one time ran a newsagent on Tyneside, is now based at the Stadium of Light as Sunderland's director of youth.

DON ROGERS
Winger
Born 25.10.45, Paulton

LEAGUE RECORD

	A	G
Swindon Town	411 (1)	148
Crystal Palace	69 (1)	28
Queen's Park Rangers	13 (5)	5

HONOURS
League Cup 1968/69

One of the best wingers in the Football League, DON ROGERS could have joined a more glamorous club but opted to spend his peak years with Swindon Town. He had joined the Robins on New Year's Eve 1960 and after impressing in the club's junior sides made his League debut in November 1962 as Swindon beat Southend United 4–1. Rogers played in just seven games that season, helping the club win promotion and scoring his first goal for the Robins in a 3–1 home win over Notts County. At the beginning of the 1963/64 season he won a regular place in the Swindon side. He scored seven goals in thirty-six games and also helped the young Robins to the final of the FA Youth Cup where they lost to Manchester United. In the close season he represented Young England in an international youth tournament in Rotterdam and was voted the 'most outstanding player' in the competition. England won the tournament, beating Spain 4–0 in the final, with Rogers scoring two of the goals.

FACT Shrewsbury Town met Swindon Town six times in 1960/61 in League, League Cup and FA Cup matches, and did not lose once. Huddersfield Town and Plymouth Argyle met six times in 1963/64 in League, League Cup and FA Cup games.

Rogers was then ever-present for the next four seasons, appearing in 181 consecutive League games. In 1964/65 he scored eighteen goals including the first of four hat-tricks for the club in a 6–0 home win over York City. He top-scored for the Robins for the first time in 1966/67 when his total of twenty-four goals included hat-tricks in the home wins over Oldham Athletic (6–3) and Middlesbrough (4–1). His best season in terms of goals scored was 1967/68, when he headed the club's scoring lists with twenty-five. He top-scored again in the club's promotion-winning season of 1968/69 when his twenty-two goals included his last hat-trick for the Robins in a 5–1 home win over Southport. That same season he scored two of Swindon's goals in the League Cup Final as Arsenal were beaten 3–1.

Rogers's performances for the Robins led to his selection for the England Under-23 side, and despite the fact that Swindon were a Third Division side he surely deserved a chance at full international level. Following the club's promotion he helped the Robins lift the Anglo-Italian Cup but in November 1972 he left the County Ground to join Crystal Palace. In his first season at Selhurst

Park he scored several brilliant televised goals but at the end of the campaign Palace were relegated and Rogers left to join Queen's Park Rangers. After eighteen appearances for the Loftus Road Club he returned to Swindon Town where he took his tally of goals to 177 in 478 League and Cup games before hanging up his boots.

Don Rogers remained in Swindon, opening up his own sports shop which he has now run for over thirty years.

PETER SIMPSON
Central Defender
Born 13.1.45, Great Yarmouth

LEAGUE RECORD

	A	G
Arsenal	353 (17)	10

HONOURS
League Championship 1970/71
FA Cup 1970/71
Inter Cities Fairs Cup 1969/70

PETER SIMPSON rose to senior status via the Highbury youth system and made his League debut at home to Chelsea in March 1964. It wasn't a happy experience as he watched his direct opponent Bobby Tambling score all four goals in the visitors' easy victory. Over the next couple of seasons Simpson made only intermittent appearances, that is until Bertie Mee was appointed manager. During the course of the 1966/67 season Simpson made thirty-six League appearances, playing these matches in virtually every position except goalkeeper. Under the new regime Simpson emerged as a more polished

defender than Terry Neill or Ian Ure. After sharing in the gloom of two League Cup reverses in 1967/68 and 1968/69, Simpson sampled glory for the first time in the 1969/70 Inter Cities Fairs Cup.

Alf Ramsey selected Simpson for the preliminary squad for the 1970 World Cup but the presence of Bobby Moore and Norman Hunter ensured that he didn't make the final 22. While no one could contend that the Gunners' left-half was the equal of the England captain, there were those who thought he was more comfortable on the ball than the Leeds United defender. Although he was called into several squads, Peter Simpson never won a full international cap and along with George Swindin and George Armstrong must be considered as one of Arsenal's best players never to win a full international cap. Strong in the air and an expert at the sliding tackle, he preferred to play his way out of trouble, relying on shrewd interception and accurate distribution.

Following Arsenal's success in the Inter Cities Fairs Cup, Simpson had to undergo a cartilage operation which sidelined him for three months. He was back to play a leading role in the Arsenal team when they achieved the 'double' in 1970/71 and he also appeared for the club in the 1972 FA Cup Final against Leeds United. From then until the 1974/75 season he held his place in the League side but spent the next three seasons in and out of the team before being released in the summer of 1978. On leaving Highbury, he went to the United States where he ended his career playing for New England Teamen and later Hendon. The commanding central defender is now working as a forklift truck driver for a roofing materials firm in Hertfordshire.

BOBBY SMITH
Centre-Forward
Born 22.2.33, Skelton

LEAGUE RECORD

	A	G
Chelsea	74	23
Tottenham Hotspur	271	176
Brighton & Hove Albion	31	19

HONOURS

League Championship 1960/61
FA Cup 1960/61 and 1961/62
Fourth Division Championship 1964/65
European Cup Winners' Cup 1962/63
15 England Caps

The son of a Yorkshire miner, BOBBY SMITH was a burly, bustling centre-forward who not only scored goals but also put the fear of God into intimidated defenders and goalkeepers. By the age of seventeen he was in Chelsea's League side, going on to score thirty goals in eighty-six games before losing his place to Roy Bentley. In December 1955 he joined the struggling Tottenham Hotspur; when Smith arrived at White Hart Lane, they were only one place off the bottom of the First Division. Smith duly scored the goals necessary to dispel the threat of relegation before going on to play an important role in the most glorious years in the club's history.

In 1957/58 he replaced Len Duquemin, and with Tommy Harmer creating numerous openings for him he scored thirty-six League goals to equal Ted Harper's 1930/31 club record. By the start of the 1960/61 season he had overtaken George Hunt's aggregate of League goals for Spurs. In October 1960 he won his first England cap against Northern Ireland, going on to score thirteen goals in fifteen games for his country.

He was top-scorer during the club's 'double'-winning season of 1960/61 and hit some crucial goals in the FA Cup, including a brace in the semi-final against Burnley and the first in the final itself against Leicester City. He was on target again the following season as Spurs retained the FA Cup. By then, he had the mercurial Jimmy Greaves playing alongside him and together they formed the most feared striking partnership in the Football League.

Despite liking nothing more than a hard, physical challenge, Bobby Smith also possessed a great deal of skill. However, there were times when Spurs manager Bill Nicholson preferred the more subtle approach of Les Allen and Smith was left out of the team. But he was always included for the more important games and when Spurs won the European Cup Winners' Cup in 1963 his presence gave the North London club a hefty psychological advantage over their Spanish opponents.

At the end of the following season Smith was allowed to leave White Hart Lane and joined Brighton and Hove Albion, his eighteen goals in thirty-one games helping the Seagulls win the Fourth Division Championship. Before the new season began he fell out with the club over comments in some newspaper articles and was sacked. He then joined Hastings United and later played for Banbury United.

After hanging up his boots, Bobby had a series of driving and labouring jobs before becoming a painter and decorator. He was increasingly troubled by the effects of several old injuries that were a painful legacy of his memorably wholehearted style of play. He had to have a double hip replacement operation and now relies on crutches to get around.

LEAGUE RECORD

	A	G
Liverpool	467	36
Swansea City	34 (2)	2

HONOURS
FA Cup 1964/65 and 1973/74
League Championship 1965/66,
   1972/73, 1975/76 and 1976/77
UEFA Cup 1972/73 and 1975/76
European Cup 1976/77
1 England Cap

TOMMY SMITH
Defender
Born 5.4.45, Liverpool

Born within a corner-kick's distance of Anfield, TOMMY SMITH grew up to become one of the club's greatest servants. He developed into one of the toughest defenders in the Football League and was club captain for a while. He made his Liverpool debut against Birmingham City in May 1963, standing in for the injured Gordon Milne.

Tommy Smith became an integral member of Bill Shankly's first great Liverpool side. He played initially in midfield before moving into the centre of defence. He had more skill than he was generally given credit for and contributed greatly to Liverpool's FA Cup success of 1965 and the ensuing Championship campaign. The obvious choice to replace Ron Yeats as captain, Smith was an inspiration, driving the team on to greater efforts. He relished the position and its responsibilities and in the 1970/71 season gave some of his best-ever performances. In that season he won his only England cap and was narrowly pipped as 'Footballer of the Year' by Arsenal's Frank McLintock. He led Liverpool to the FA Cup Final in 1971 when they lost to Arsenal, before leading the Reds to a unique 'double' of League Championship and UEFA Cup in 1972/73. He was dropped in November 1973, resulting in a heated discussion with Bill Shankly, this confrontation losing him the captaincy to Emlyn Hughes. He almost moved to Stoke City but returned to the Liverpool team to replace the injured Chris Lawler at right-back. After winning several more trophies he began to be troubled by knee problems and announced his retirement in early 1977.

Match of the Day was first screened on 22 August 1964. The very first programme lasted forty-five minutes and showed highlights of a game between Liverpool and Arsenal. Liverpool won 3–2.

FACT

However, not long afterwards Phil Thompson was injured and Smith found himself back in the centre of the Liverpool defence. He had a superb season, facing Manchester United at Wembley in the FA Cup Final, winning another League Championship medal and then making his 600th appearance in a Liverpool shirt in the European Cup Final against Borussia Moenchengladbach. The veteran of so many past glories, Smith rose majestically to meet Heighway's corner and send a header of immense power crashing into the Germans' net. He

stayed at Anfield for another season and would probably have played against Bruges in the European Cup Final but he dropped a pick-axe on his foot! Though he was offered a one-year contract, Smith joined John Toshack at Swansea, who made him a better offer. He later made a brief return to Anfield as coach to the club's youth team.

Tommy Smith was a player of great courage, toughness and determination, and he will go down in football folklore as one of the hardest men the game has known. He is still involved with the Reds in a public relations capacity.

LEAGUE RECORD

	A	G
Leeds United	381	0
Birmingham City	16	0

HONOURS
Second Division Championship 1963/64
League Cup 1967/68
League Championship 1968/69
Inter Cities Fairs Cup 1967/68 and 1970/71
37 Wales Caps

GARY SPRAKE
Goalkeeper
Born 3.4.45, Swansea

GARY SPRAKE lived next door but one to Arsenal and Wales goalkeeper Jack Kelsey. Sprake too was capped by his country, becoming Wales's youngest-ever goalkeeper when he made his debut against Scotland in November 1963 aged 18 years and 231 days.

Sprake left school at the age of fifteen to take an apprenticeship as a fitter and turner, playing in goal for the works team in his spare time. He was spotted by Leeds United's Welsh scout Jack Pickard, who also discovered John Charles playing for Swansea Schools. In March 1962 Sprake made an unexpected first-team debut for the Elland Road club. He was enjoying a lie-in when frantic Leeds officials contacted him on the morning of

> During the game between Leeds and Liverpool in December 1967 Gary Sprake decided at the last minute not to throw the ball out to a colleague. However, momentum took the ball out of his hand and it ended up in his own net.
>
> **FACT**

United's Second Division game at Southampton. The club's first-choice keeper Tommy Younger had been taken ill and so sixteen-year-old Sprake was rushed to Manchester's Ringway Airport and flown to the south coast on a two-seater plane for a dramatic League debut. The game kicked off fifteen minutes late because of United's predicament and although the Saints won 4–1 Sprake had made a good impression and the following season took Younger's place on merit.

Leeds manager Don Revie thought very highly of Sprake and when the young keeper, homesick and losing his confidence, abandoned Elland Road to return to South Wales, Revie followed him to convince the blond-haired six-footer that he had a real future in the game. Sprake made the breakthrough into the Leeds first team in September 1962 in the match against Swansea at the Vetch Field, a game the Yorkshire club won 2–0. He was the Leeds' first-choice keeper for the next ten seasons, during which time he won a League Championship medal, a League Cup winners' medal, two Inter Cities Fairs Cup medals and a Division Two Championship medal.

When Leeds took the League Championship in 1968/69, Sprake was ever-present as the Elland Road club won the title with the fewest number of goals conceded by any champions. At the start of the season Sprake produced heroics to keep out Ferencvaros of Hungary and help Leeds secure a goalless draw and so win the Inter Cities Fairs Cup for the first time. A member of the phenomenal Leeds side of the 1970s, Sprake played in 507 first-team games. Although he was an acrobatic and exciting keeper, he was also prone to lapses of concentration, more often than not when television cameras were present.

After losing his place to David Harvey, Sprake was transferred to Birmingham City in October 1973. He had made just sixteen appearances for the St Andrew's club when injury and illness forced his premature retirement from the game. He worked briefly as a representative for a sports goods firm in Solihull but now works for the local council as a training officer, responsible for placing business trainees and monitoring their progress.

LEAGUE RECORD

	A	G
Millwall	137	0
Chelsea	1	0
Manchester United	433	2

HONOURS
League Championship 1966/67
Second Division Championship 1974/75
FA Cup 1976/77
European Cup 1967/68
1 England Cap

ALEX STEPNEY
Goalkeeper
Born 18.9.42, Mitcham

Of all the goalkeepers in Manchester United's long history, ALEX STEPNEY will always rank among the most popular and respected. A solid, secure and unspectacular keeper, he began his career with non-League Tooting and Mitcham before turning professional with Millwall in 1963. He had made almost 150 appearances for the Lions when in May 1966 Tommy Docherty signed him for Chelsea for £50,000. Stepney made just one League appearance for Chelsea before being transferred four months later to United for £55,000. At least Chelsea made a profit, but given the magnificent service that Stepney gave to United the Blues might later have regretted not giving him a little more encouragement.

Stepney immediately replaced Dave Gaskell in the United side and made his League debut in front of 62,085 fans in the Manchester 'derby', as a Denis Law goal gave United a 1–0 win. In his first season at Old Trafford, United lifted the League Championship and then in 1967/68 the European Cup. It was the heroics of Alex Stepney, with two instinctive saves from Eusebio in the closing minutes of normal time, which kept United alive in the final against Benfica. The extra time goals will always be the highlight of their famous victory but Stepney's part should never be forgotten.

He went on to play in 535 League and Cup games for United and even scored a couple of goals from the penalty-spot in the Reds' relegation season of 1973/74 – Leicester City (Home 1–2) and Birmingham City (Home 1–0) – and at one point he was actually the club's leading goalscorer! He won a Second Division Championship medal to add to his League Championship medal and later won an FA Cup winners' medal when United beat Liverpool 2–1 at Wembley in 1977 to deny the Anfield club the 'double'.

Stepney was capped just once by England in 1968 against Sweden and although he was also chosen for the 1970 World Cup squad he never actually played. After twelve seasons' loyal service, he left United and went to play in the United States with Dallas Tornadoes and then later returned to Britain to play non-League football for Altrincham.

After retiring, Stepney had a spell as commercial manager at Rochdale, having previously held a variety of jobs, including running a pub, managing a van hire business in Rochdale and working in a car body repair shop. He is now goalkeeping coach at newly promoted Manchester City.

NOBBY STILES
Wing-Half
Born 18.5.42, Manchester

LEAGUE RECORD

	A	G
Manchester United	311	17
Middlesbrough	57	2
Preston North End	44 (2)	1

HONOURS
League Championship 1964/65 and 1966/67
European Cup 1967/68
28 England Caps

The image of toothless terrier NOBBY STILES dancing round Wembley with the World Cup after England's 1966 win is an unforgettable soccer memory. Stiles, who played a great part in England's 4–2 win over West Germany, was a Manchester United apprentice at the time of the Munich Air Disaster, going on to make his League debut against Bolton Wanderers in October 1960. He shared in United's successful 1963 FA Cup run, though he didn't win a place in the final. Shortly afterwards he became firmly established in the United side and hardly missed a match in 1966/67 when the Reds won the League Championship.

It has been said that many of Nobby's awkward-looking tackles in the early days were probably because he wasn't wearing his spectacles, and that his tackling only improved after he was fitted with contact lenses! After United won the European Cup in 1968, Nobby's standing in the game was at a peak, but his earlier bad boy image was reflected by his pen picture in the match programme when the Reds played Estudiantes in the World Club Championship: he was described as 'brutal, badly intentional and a bad sportsman'. The fans abroad certainly didn't like Nobby, for in his time he was called an assassin in South America, was spat at in Italy and hit on the head by a bottle in Madrid. Playing without his false teeth made him look like Dracula and according to the French, who met him in the 1966 World Cup tournament, he was twice as dangerous!

Stiles had a reputation for fierce tackling. His aggressive play as a wing-half earned him the respect of team-mates and opponents alike. He may have been small in stature but his heart was big. Known to his team-mates as 'Happy', he worked hard for the team, his enthusiasm rubbing off on others.

At the age of twenty-seven he underwent two cartilage operations and in May 1971 United accepted a £320,000 offer from Middlesbrough. After two seasons at Ayresome Park, Stiles moved to Preston North End to play for Bobby Charlton. He only played for one more season but spent a further seven years at Deepdale, three as coach and the last four as manager. On leaving North End, he teamed up with his brother-in-law Johnny Giles, Nobby becoming coach at Vancouver Whitecaps. He followed Giles to the Hawthorns to do a similar job for West Bromwich Albion but in 1988 he returned to old Trafford to coach United's youngsters.

As co-director of United's School of Excellence, Nobby Stiles is now a perennially popular speaker on the after-dinner circuit.

LEAGUE RECORD

	A	G
Liverpool	334 (2)	95
Coventry City	18	3
Tranmere Rovers	9	1

HONOURS
League Championship 1963/64
  and 1965/66
Second Division Championship 1964/65
FA Cup 1964/65
21 Scotland Caps

IAN ST JOHN
Forward
Born 7.6.38, Motherwell

After paying Motherwell £37,500 for IAN ST JOHN, nicknamed the Saint, Bill Shankly described him as the man the Reds couldn't afford not to buy, and the most urgently needed component of his new team. In 1959, while playing for the Fir Park Club, St John had set a new record for the fastest hat-trick in Scottish football, netting three goals in the space of two-and-a-half minutes! His first appearance in a Liverpool shirt was against Everton in a Senior Cup Final at Goodison Park in August 1961 and he was an instant hit with the fans as he scored a hat-trick.

St John was strong, courageous and quite devastating in the air for a man of 5ft 7in. His delicate flicks did much to promote a fine understanding with Roger Hunt – St John scored eighteen goals that first season as the Reds won promotion. During that Division Two title campaign St John often showed flashes of bad temper and in March 1962 he was sent off with Preston's Tony Singleton after such a clash. Fire, though, was an integral part of the Saint's make-up. His first season in the top flight saw him score nineteen goals and then twenty-one in 1963/64 as Liverpool went on to win the Championship. During that campaign Liverpool's scheming inside-forward Jimmy Melia was injured and Shanks withdrew St John into a deep-lying role. He fulfilled his true potential in this position and became the mastermind of the Reds' attack. He gave his team-mates plenty of possession and created space for them with his intelligent running. It certainly wasn't the end of his goals, his jack-knife header against Leeds United at Wembley in 1965 winning the FA Cup.

As his fitness began to decline, St John was used a little more sparingly. On the substitute's bench for the Inter Cities Fairs Cup tie against Dynamo Bucharest, he was brought into the game with Liverpool holding a precarious 1–0 lead. With his sure touch and close passing skills, he laid on two goals near the end of the match to leave the Reds comfortable winners at 3–0.

The Saint was a tough and tenacious player, representing Scotland on twenty-one occasions. On leaving Anfield he had short spells with Coventry City and Tranmere Rovers before going into coaching and then management. He didn't succeed as much as many people thought he might. Eventually he became a television personality, sharing the screen with another great goalscorer from the

1960s, Jimmy Greaves. However, it is not as Greavsie's chat-show partner that the Saint should be recalled, but as a crucial piece of the Liverpool jigsaw that has seen success over the last four decades.

LEAGUE RECORD

	A	G
Nottingham Forest	235 (1)	105
Manchester United	39	11

HONOURS
1 England Cap

IAN STOREY-MOORE

Winger
Born 17.1.45, Ipswich

IAN STOREY-MOORE is the only professional footballer with a double-barrelled name to have played for England though he preferred to be known simply as 'Ian Moore'. A fast, hard-shooting winger, he had trials with Scunthorpe United before joining Nottingham Forest as an amateur in 1961, turning professional in May 1962. Though he made his Football League debut in May 1963 as Forest beat his home-town club Ipswich Town 2–1 at the City Ground, it took a little time for him to become a first-team regular.

A brilliant, exciting player, Storey-Moore was a lethal finisher and was Forest's top-scorer in 1966/67, 1968/69, 1969/70, 1970/71 and 1971/72, even though he left the club in February 1972! His best season in terms of goals scored was 1966/67, when he netted twenty-five League and Cup goals including a hat-trick in a 3–2 defeat of Everton in an FA Cup sixth-round tie. His other hat-trick for the City Ground club came in March 1971 as Crystal Palace were beaten 3–1.

There is no doubt that if it hadn't been for Alf Ramsey's policy of not playing wingers, Storey-Moore would have won more than the one England cap he gained against Holland in 1970. In ten years at Forest he netted 118 goals in 272 League and Cup games, before being transferred to Manchester United for £200,000 in March 1972, following a controversial episode at Derby when the Rams' then assistant-manager Peter Taylor, believing that Storey-Moore was *their* player, introduced him to the crowd before a League match at the Baseball Ground. But although Storey-Moore had signed the forms, Forest secretary Ken Smales had not, because the Forest committee were concerned that another of their players, Terry Hennessey, had done well at Derby, Forest's neighbours and deadly rivals. They refused to let Storey-Moore go to Derby – who were fined over the incident – and instead sold him to United.

Storey-Moore's career at Old Trafford was plagued by injuries and eventually he was forced out of League football in 1974 following an ankle injury, aggravated in United's gymnasium. He moved back to the East Midlands with his insurance money and made a comeback in non-League football, initially with Burton Albion and then Shepshed Charterhouse. He also appeared for Chicago Stings in the NASL. Since hanging up his boots he has become a successful businessman in Nottingham, where he runs a pub and owns a bookmakers. A fully qualified FA coach, he also works for Nottingham Forest.

MIKE SUMMERBEE

Winger
Born 15.12.42, Cheltenham

LEAGUE RECORD

	A	G
Swindon Town	218	39
Manchester City	355 (2)	47
Burnley	51	0
Blackpool	3	0
Stockport County	86 (1)	6

HONOURS
Second Division Championship
  1965/66
League Championship 1967/68
FA Cup 1968/69
League Cup 1969/70
8 England Caps

MIKE SUMMERBEE was a West Country boy from a footballing family, his uncle George having been a professional with Chester, Preston and Barrow. When he left school, he played for his home-town club Cheltenham until Swindon Town spotted his potential. He played in more than two hundred games for the Wiltshire club, helping them clinch promotion from Division Three in 1962/63. Inevitably his dashing excursions along the wings caught the eye of some of the bigger clubs and in August 1965 he became the first of Joe Mercer's signings when Manchester City paid £30,000 for his services.

After making his City debut in a 1–1 draw at Middlesbrough, he went on in his first season to help them win the Second Division title and then in a three-year spell between 1968 and 1970 – the most successful period in the club's history – he played a significant role in City's triumphs. Though he wasn't a prolific goalscorer, he did hit a hat-trick in the club's 7–0 FA Cup win over Reading at Elm Park after the first match at Maine Road had ended goalless. Primarily right-footed, he made an immediate impression at Maine Road with his diligence and industry. He always tackled back and shouldered his share of the defensive duties – he was a hard, uncompromising player.

In the FA Cup Final of 1969 it was Summerbee who stormed down the right wing, avoiding the challenges of Nish and Woollett, to cut the ball back from the dead-ball line for Neil Young to strike home the only goal of the game. He certainly enjoyed the limelight. A confident player on the field, deputising as a central striker when the club had injuries, he was a fashionable dresser off it and part-owner of a boutique with Manchester United's George Best. He won eight full caps for England, making his debut against Scotland in 1968.

Summerbee spent ten seasons with Manchester City before he moved to Turf Moor in June 1975. His career later took him to Blackpool and then to Edgeley Park, where he combined his role on the field with that of manager. These days Mike Summerbee is actively working with the commercial department at Manchester City, as well as running his own shirt-making business which boasts clients such as Michael Caine and Sylvester Stallone! He is also an after-dinner speaker and with his background it will surely be some time before he runs out of tales to tell.

LEAGUE RECORD

	A	G
Chelsea	298 (4)	164
Crystal Palace	67 (1)	12

HONOURS
League Cup 1964/65
3 England Caps

BOBBY TAMBLING
Forward
Born 18.9.41, Storrington

BOBBY TAMBLING had his first taste of League football as a seventeen-year-old for Chelsea against West Ham United in February 1959 and, like his fellow debutant Barry Bridges, he scored in a 3–2 win. But it was 1960/61 before he began to appear for the Blues on a regular basis, initially at left-wing and then at inside-forward.

When Jimmy Greaves left Stamford Bridge and headed for Italy in the summer of 1961, Tambling was thrust into the limelight. Despite the burden placed on his young shoulders, he emerged from Chelsea's grim battle against relegation as the club's top scorer with twenty goals in thirty-four appearances. The following season, at the age of twenty-one, he became the youngest player to have captained a promotion-winning side, when he was appointed to succeed Peter Sillett. Leading from the front, he ended that 1962/63 season with thirty-five League goals, twenty-five of them in the twenty-two games he played before the 'Big Freeze' interrupted the Blues' rhythm. Towards the end of the season he scored four goals against Portsmouth when victory was essential to clinch promotion. Not surprisingly, his outstanding form earned him full England honours against Wales and France.

During the opening weeks of the 1963/64 season Tambling found goals hard to come by and on the advice of manager Tommy Docherty he relinquished the captaincy to Ken Shellito. As his career progressed, he did not enjoy the best of luck with injuries, suffering a hamstring strain in 1965/66 and abdominal problems requiring surgery on two occasions a couple of seasons later. A cartilage operation cost him his first-team place at the start of the 1969/70 season.

Tambling scored four goals for Chelsea on four occasions and managed five goals in a game against Aston Villa in 1966. Some of his goals were highly spectacular, perhaps none more so than the stunning free-kick he swerved round the defensive wall in an FA Cup fifth-round match against Sheffield Wednesday in 1968. An integral member of the Chelsea side during the

FACT

On 21 May 1963 Chelsea gained Division One status by beating Portsmouth 7–0 at Stamford Bridge, skipper Bobby Tambling scoring four of the goals. Four minutes from time hundreds of exultant spectators swarmed on to the pitch, bringing play to a halt and risking an abandonment of the match. But the field was cleared and the final whistle produced another invasion. Chelsea had succeeded in obtaining second place in Division Two on goal average, with 1.928 compared to Sunderland's 1.527.

most successful decade in the club's history, his total of 202 goals remains a club record.

Unable to regain his first-team place after his cartilage operation, owing to the formidable partnership of Ian Hutchinson and Peter Osgood, he joined Crystal Palace on a month's loan. He made the switch a permanent one and stayed at Selhurst Park for four seasons before going to play for a number of Irish clubs including Cork Celtic, Waterford and Shamrock Rovers.

For many years after hanging up his boots he ran a sports shop in Havant and then worked as a hod carrier. Bobby Tambling now lives in Ireland.

PETER THOMPSON
Winger
Born 27.11.42, Carlisle

LEAGUE RECORD	A	G
Preston North End	121	20
Liverpool	318 (4)	41
Bolton Wanderers	111 (6)	2

HONOURS
League Championship 1963/64 and 1965/66
FA Cup 1964/65
16 England Caps

PETER THOMPSON began his career with Preston North End, and turned professional in the year the legendary Tom Finney retired. He soon established himself as one of Preston's most consistent performers and in August 1963, in the face of competition from Everton, Wolves and Juventus, Bill Shankly paid £40,000 to bring him to Anfield. After an impressive debut against Blackburn Rovers at Ewood Park, where he forced the Rovers' defenders to twist and turn in their efforts to stay with him, Thompson became a great favourite with the Reds' supporters. At the end of his first full season Liverpool won the League Championship and Thompson gave his best display of the campaign in a 5–0 rout of Arsenal, scoring twice as the Reds made certain of the title.

There were those who said Thompson should have scored more goals. Certainly, when he did score, they were often spectacular and match-winners. The accuracy of his crosses played an important part in establishing Roger Hunt as one of the most feared goalscorers of the time and in 1965/66 it was no coincidence that Thompson played in forty games and Hunt scored twenty-seven goals.

Making his international debut against Portugal in 1964, Thompson was a regular in the England side for the next two years, though he was a victim of Alf Ramsey's decision to play the 1966 World Cup without wingers. Peter Thompson was a fantastic winger: he could take on defenders in tight situations and go past them with ease, and had great speed and superb ball control. He collected two League Championship medals and an FA Cup winners' medal with Liverpool. However, after being plagued by knee trouble, Thompson found himself languishing in the Reds' reserve side and in November 1973 he moved to Bolton Wanderers on loan. Though he had been considering retirement, he made his debut for the Wanderers against Second Division leaders Sunderland in a game played on a Wednesday afternoon because of a power strike. Bolton won 1–0 and the fans took Thompson to their hearts immediately. In January 1974 he signed for the club for £18,000 – one of the best bargain buys of all time. His displays on the wing guided Bolton through one of their most exciting periods, culminating in promotion to Division One.

Thompson retired in April 1978. After running two caravan parks for a number of years, he moved to the Lake District to run a country pub. He recently moved to Harrogate to run a hotel.

TERRY VENABLES
Midfielder
Born 6.1.43, Dagenham

LEAGUE RECORD

	A	G
Chelsea	202	26
Tottenham Hotspur	114 (1)	5
Queen's Park Rangers	176 (1)	19
Crystal Palace	14	0

HONOURS
League Cup 1964/65
FA Cup 1966/67
2 England Caps

From schoolboy star to England manager, TERRY VENABLES' rise through all levels of football has been nothing short of mercurial. An England Schools, Youth and Amateur international, he first showed his footballing talent as a member of Tommy Docherty's young Chelsea team that won promotion to the First Division in 1962/63 and the League Cup in 1964/65. Having won four Under-23 caps, his selection for the full England team against Belgium in October 1964 made him the first player to win international honours at all levels. He also played for the Football League against the Irish League the same month, but won only one more cap, against Holland in December 1964. In May 1966 he was transferred to Tottenham Hotspur for £80,000. Though he wasn't the most fluid or swiftest mover on the ball, he had accurate passing skills – especially at long range – and great vision for productive forward openings.

In his first season with Spurs he won an FA Cup winners' medal against his old club Chelsea, but overall he had quite a difficult time at White Hart Lane. He was a virtual ever-present for three seasons but at the time Spurs were in a transitional stage and memories of the superb 'double' side were still far too vivid. Although he made every effort to do so, Venables never really won over the hearts of Spurs' supporters. Towards the end of his time at White Hart Lane he was a victim of intolerance and some fierce abuse and it was only after his £70,000 transfer to Queen's Park Rangers that his true value and influence were really appreciated. He captained Rangers to promotion to the First Division as runners-up to Burnley in 1972/73 but after one season in the top flight he left Loftus Road to play for Crystal Palace.

After only fourteen games he retired to become coach at Selhurst Park but when Malcolm Allison left Venables took over as manager and in his first season led the Eagles to promotion from Division Three. In 1978/79 Palace were Second Division champions, but two years later Venables resigned and rejoined Queen's Park Rangers. In 1982 he led the club to their first-ever FA Cup Final, and the

FACT
Terry Venables was best man at the wedding of George and Marie Graham in September 1967. The same afternoon the groom and his best man played for Arsenal and Tottenham Hotspur respectively in the North London derby.

following year they won the Second Division Championship. Lured away by Barcelona, Venables led the Spanish club to the League title and to the European Cup Final but later resigned to return to England and manage Spurs. His contribution at White Hart Lane was always full of incident and culminated in a public conflict with Alan Sugar. His eventual dismissal provoked fierce protest among the fans but in 1994 he was appointed England coach, leading the team to the semi-finals of the 1996 European Championships. After giving way to Glenn Hoddle, he had spells as Portsmouth's club chairman and as head coach of Crystal Palace before helping preserve Middlesbrough's Premiership status. A regular face on ITV's *Premiership* programme, Venables joined Leeds United as manager in 2002.

ROY VERNON

Inside-Forward
Born 14.4.37, Prestatyn
Died 4.12.93

LEAGUE RECORD

	A	G
Blackburn Rovers	131	49
Everton	176	101
Stoke City	84 (3)	22
Halifax Town	4	0

HONOURS
League Championship 1962/63
32 Wales Caps

One of Ewood Park's 'Carey Chicks', ROY VERNON made his League debut for Blackburn Rovers in September 1955 in a 3–3 home draw against Liverpool. By the time he was nineteen, Vernon had won full international honours, playing for Wales against Northern Ireland. A creative player who struck a dead ball with tremendous power and great accuracy, Vernon was a member of the Welsh side that reached the quarter-finals of the 1958 World Cup Finals in Sweden. He began

to grow disillusioned with life at Ewood Park and in February 1960 followed his mentor, Johnny Carey, to Everton for a fee of £27,000. Although he didn't realise it at the time, Vernon robbed himself of a Wembley appearance with this move.

Vernon made his Everton debut in a 2–0 home defeat at the hands of Wolverhampton Wanderers, going on to score nine goals in the final twelve games of the season. In 1960/61 he was the club's leading scorer with twenty-one goals, including a hat-trick in a 4–1 win over Arsenal on the final day of the season. In 1961/62 he was again the club's top scorer with twenty-six goals in thirty-seven League outings, including another treble in an 8–3 rout of Cardiff City. Vernon set about his work with compelling efficiency and skippered the Blues to the League Championship in 1962/63, netting another hat-trick in a 4–1 win over Fulham as the Toffees clinched the title. Vernon went on to score 110 goals in 199 League and Cup games for Everton before moving to Stoke City in March 1965.

Vernon eventually won thirty-two caps for Wales. When he lost his place in the Stoke side after five productive years with the Potters, he moved to Halifax Town where he ended his Football League career. He returned to Lancashire in 1970 to join former Blackburn team-mates Ronnie Clayton and Bryan Douglas at Great Harwood, helping to take the Northern Premier League side into the first round of the FA Cup for the first time.

Vernon retired from the game in 1972. He then ran an antiques business in Blackburn but began to suffer with arthritis of the hip and spine. He died in December 1993 at the early age of fifty-six.

LEAGUE RECORD

	A	G
Blackpool	257	0
Burnley	38	0

HONOURS
5 England Caps

TONY WAITERS
Goalkeeper
Born 1.2.37, Southport

TONY WAITERS was almost twenty-three years old when he turned professional with Blackpool in October 1959 and had already represented England as an amateur while at Loughborough College. He joined the Seasiders, initially as an amateur, from the Cheshire League club Macclesfield in the summer of 1959. Veteran Scottish international keeper George Farm had been a permanent fixture between the posts for Blackpool for over a decade, but after making his debut against Blackburn Rovers on Boxing Day 1959, Waiters made the no. 1 jersey his. Tall, well-built and supremely fit, Tony Waiters was one of the country's top goalkepers in the early 1960s but competition at the highest level was fierce indeed, notably from Ron Springett and the immaculate Gordon Banks.

Waiters won his first representative honour at professional level in October 1963 when he was selected for a Football League XI to face the League of Ireland in Dublin. Then in May 1964 he won the first of five full international caps, also in Dublin,

In 1967/68 Birmingham City dropped the idea of reproducing pictures of Blues' players taking penalty-kicks following a miss by Malcolm Beard in the game against Blackpool. The Seasiders' goalkeeper Alan Taylor had noticed a picture showing Beard scoring with a left-footed shot to the keeper's right. Taylor chose the same way and saved the goal. Blackpool won 2–1.

FACT

performing solidly in a 3–1 win. His second international appearance came a week later in the giant Maracana Stadium in Rio de Janeiro and, with Pele in outstanding form, Waiters could do little more than admire as the World Champions cruised home 5–1.

All of Tony Waiters' Blackpool career was in the top flight but after the Seasiders were relegated in 1967 he decided to retire, becoming the Football Association's north-west regional coach. In January 1969 he became youth coach at Liverpool but in the summer of 1970 he joined Burnley in a similar position, also acting as understudy to goalkeeper Peter Mellor. Within two weeks of Waiters' arrival, Mellor had dislocated a shoulder during training; Waiters stepped up to resume his First Division career at the age of thirty-three, and more than three years after his last Football League appearance. He was the Clarets' regular keeper during the 1970/71 season, a campaign which saw Burnley lose their top-flight status. In December 1971 he retired once more, this time joining Coventry City as their director of coaching.

After a spell as England Youth Team manager, he spent almost five years as manager of Plymouth Argyle, leading the Pilgrims to promotion to the Third Division in 1974/75. Following a number of successful years as the coach of Vancouver Whitecaps in the NASL, he was appointed coach to the Canadian National Team. He still lives in Canada, where he now runs his own soccer school.

GORDON WEST

Goalkeeper
Born 24.4.43, Darfield, Yorkshire

LEAGUE RECORD

	A	G
Blackpool	31	0
Everton	335	0
Tranmere Rovers	17	0

HONOURS

League Championship 1962/63 and
  1969/70
FA Cup 1965/66
3 England Caps

Though he had trials with several clubs as a schoolboy centre-half, GORDON WEST was a natural goalkeeper. He made his First Division debut for Blackpool as a seventeen-year-old, temporarily replacing Tony Waiters in the Seasiders' team and his performances for the Bloomfield Road club led to Everton manager Harry Catterick handing over £27,000, then a record fee for a goalkeeper, to make West his first signing as the Blues' boss. It was certainly a bold move but one that paid dividends, for in 1962/63, his first full season, West replaced Albert Dunlop in goal and helped the Blues win the League Championship, keeping seventeen clean sheets in his thirty-eight appearances. However,

> **FACT**
>
> Mike Trebilcock scored twice for Everton in the 1966 FA Cup Final, despite the fact that his name wasn't printed in the official match programme.

over the next couple of seasons West shared the goalkeeping duties with the ever-improving Andy Rankin before reasserting himself on the club's 1966 Wembley trail. In the seven matches on the way to the final West didn't concede a single goal and was outstanding in the games against Coventry and Manchester City.

Though West was one of the most flamboyant characters of the Catterick era, the dressing-room joker, he was also notoriously nervous prior to a game. He enjoyed a particularly warm relationship with Liverpool fans, to whom he endeared himself by blowing them a kiss after a torrent of abuse. The Kop's response was to present him with a handbag! West's humour also shone through in the game against Newcastle United in October 1967, a match the Blues lost 1–0. The Everton keeper had been sent off for punching the Magpies' forward Albert Bennett and was replaced between the posts by Sandy Brown. After the final whistle West had his team-mates in stitches as he berated poor Sandy for failing to save the resulting penalty!

Following Everton's FA Cup win, West missed very few games over the following four seasons, picking up a second League Championship medal in 1969/70. His consistency brought him to the attention of Sir Alf Ramsey but West astonished the football world when he refused to join the England party for the 1970 World Cup Finals in Mexico, preferring to remain at home with his family.

In 1970/71 West fell out of favour but again confounded the doubters by returning to be ever-present the following season. However, after David Lawson arrived from Huddersfield Town, West made only four League appearances before deciding to retire. Two years later he was lured back to the game by Tranmere Rovers. After shedding some weight he provided the Prenton Park club with four seasons of first-team cover.

He later became a member of the groundstaff at the Wirral-based club and then went to work in security on Merseyside. Though he never quite scaled the heights predicted for him, he was without doubt one of the First Division's leading keepers throughout the 1960s.

LEAGUE RECORD		
	A	G
Arsenal	234	0

HONOURS
League Championship 1970/71
FA Cup 1970/71
Inter Cities Fairs Cup 1969/70
2 Scotland Caps

BOB WILSON
Goalkeeper
Born 30.10.41, Chesterfield

While BOB WILSON was training to become a Physical Education teacher at Loughborough College, he played as an amateur with Wolverhampton Wanderers. During the summer of 1963 he joined Arsenal and, still an amateur, made his League debut against Nottingham Forest in October of that year. However, the following season the Gunners signed Jim Furnell and Wilson had to be content to spend his first season at Highbury in the reserves. In the spring of 1964 the Gunners offered him a professional contract but he still couldn't force his way into Arsenal's first team.

In fact, in those early days Wilson, who was one of a number of Arsenal goalkeepers aspiring to become the long-term replacement for Welsh international Jack Kelsey, was prone to errors, particularly when dealing with crosses. However, after Furnell made a costly mistake against Birmingham City in the FA Cup fifth-round tie in March 1968, Wilson took over and played the last thirteen League matches of the 1968/69 season. After that, he became the inspirational last line of defence that the Gunners had lacked for half a decade, commanding his penalty area calmly and reading the game astutely – in stark contrast to his earlier displays. In 1968/69 Wilson was instrumental in Arsenal's seasonal defensive record, conceding only twenty-seven goals in forty matches. He played a major part in the 1969/70 Inter Cities Fairs Cup triumph but it was during the following campaign that he reached his peak.

He played in all of the club's sixty-four games during that 'double' winning season, and his brilliance between the posts prevented a number of games from slipping away. During the FA Cup Final against Liverpool, though, his clanger in allowing Steve Heighway to score at his near post was magnified unfairly, while two outstanding saves that kept Arsenal hopes alive were invariably forgotten. The Chesterfield-born keeper, whose parentage enabled him to win two caps for Scotland later that year, missed the 1972 final through injury. He returned for two more seasons of exemplary performances before surprisingly announcing his retirement in May 1974, at the age of only thirty-two. There is no doubt that he could have played on longer but, with the future in mind, he made the typically sensible decision to accept a television job. Though his initial screen appearances were rather shaky, his experience has brought increased appeal and authority.

In 1994 Wilson, who had a spell as Arsenal's goalkeeping coach and now runs a goalkeeping school, left the BBC, signing a contract with Carlton.

RAY WILSON

Left-Back
Born 17.12.34, Shirebrook

LEAGUE RECORD

	A	G
Huddersfield Town	266	6
Everton	114 (2)	0
Oldham Athletic	25	0
Bradford City	2	0

HONOURS

FA Cup 1965/66
63 England Caps

RAY WILSON had no burning ambition to be a professional footballer but he did play for his local youth club in the Derbyshire mining village of Shirebrook. One day when the youth club had no game Ray was asked to turn out for an open-age side – and scored all his team's goals in a 6–3 defeat. He was asked to go for a trial with Huddersfield Town and they immediately offered him terms as an apprentice professional.

When he returned from National Service in 1955 Wilson was still playing at inside-left; it was Huddersfield coach Ray Goodall who switched him with great success to full-back. Over the next few years Wilson went on to establish himself as one of the best defenders in the game, despite the fact that the Terriers were an average Second Division club.

Wilson joined Everton in the summer of 1964 in a £50,000 deal that took Mick Meagan in the opposite direction. He was now twenty-nine and already had 283 League and Cup games under his belt with Huddersfield. He had already played thirty times for England and was regarded as the best left-back in Europe. He helped the Blues win the FA Cup at Sheffield Wednesday's expense and was to return to Wembley within a matter of months to play his part in England's sensational World Cup triumph. He went on to play for Everton in the 1968 FA Cup Final, which Everton lost to West Bromwich Albion.

A competent defender, Wilson was composed and looked in command even in the most difficult of situations. He always played to his strengths and if he did have a weakness it was his heading. Ray will never forget his headed clearance that gifted Haller the opening goal of the 1966 World Cup Final. From that moment on, though, he never put a foot wrong. He won sixty-three caps for England, which stood as a record for a full-back for almost twenty years, until it was finally surpassed by Kenny Sansom.

In May 1969 Wilson was given a free transfer. He had twisted his knee prior to the start of the 1968/69 campaign and though he tried to come back as the season progressed it never felt right and he had to leave the top flight. He joined Oldham Athletic and twelve months later, in the summer of 1970, he was appointed Bradford City's youth team coach. He later worked as assistant-manager and caretaker boss. In December 1971, a month after playing his final match, he joined his brother-in-law in the family joinery and undertaking business at Outline near Huddersfield, though he has now retired.

TOMMY WRIGHT
Full-Back
Born 21.10.44, Liverpool

HONOURS
FA Cup 1965/66
League Championship 1969/70
11 England Caps

A classic case of a local boy made good, TOMMY WRIGHT joined Everton straight from school as a talented inside-forward. In the early 1960s he was a member of the Blues' 'A' side, playing in midfield alongside John Hurst and Colin Harvey. Unfortunately he was not making the progress required of him and it was only after injuries prompted a reshuffle and he found himself at right-back that he began to impress. By the middle of the 1964/65 season Wright had joined the club's senior ranks as the long-term replacement for the strong-tackling Alex Parker.

Wright was a shrewd tactician who delighted his front men with his constructive passing and pin-point crosses from his forays down the flank. One of the Blues' most dangerous attacking moves involved winger Jimmy Husband cutting inside to leave a gap for the no. 2 to charge into before picking out the head of Joe Royle. Though Wright enjoyed getting forward, such was his athleticism that he rarely got stranded upfield.

Having clawed back a two-goal deficit in the 1966 FA Cup Final against Sheffield Wednesday, the Blues had just taken the lead when Wright began to suffer with chronic cramp. With time running out the Owls attacked down their left flank, desperate for an equalising goal. The Blues' defence were at sixes and sevens and Wright was the only player in a position to give chase. Ignoring the obvious pain he was in, he sprinted to make the interception and cleared the ball with the minimum of fuss. His form was such that after playing for England at Under-23 level, he won his first full international honours against Russia in the European Championships of 1968. He went on to represent his country in the 1970 World Cup Finals in Mexico, where in the match against Brazil he had an outstanding game.

Despite taking a number of knocks, usually to his knees, Wright missed very few games and between 1966 and 1971 he was absent for only seven League games. When the Blues won the League Championship in 1969/70 Wright was one of four ever-presents, his only goal of the campaign securing two vital points in the match against Nottingham Forest.

Wright was still at his peak when, at the end of the 1972/73 season, he was forced into premature retirement at the age of twenty-nine, following recurring knee trouble. Wright, whose nephew Billy followed him into the Everton side towards the end of the decade, will always be remembered as one of football's natural gentlemen. Still following the Blues, Tommy Wright now works in the docks at Garston.

RON YEATS

Centre-Half
Born 15.11.37, Aberdeen

LEAGUE RECORD

	A	G
Liverpool	357 (1)	13
Tranmere Rovers	96 (1)	5

HONOURS
Second Division Championship 1961/62
League Championship 1963/64 and
  1965/66
FA Cup 1964/65
2 Scotland Caps

Early in his career RON YEATS had caught the eye of Bill Shankly, whose admiration for the 6ft 2in Scot dated back to when he was manager of Huddersfield Town. He had attempted to sign Yeats from Dundee United then, but the Yorkshire club could not afford the asking price. Installed at Anfield, Shankly failed in his attempt to bring Jack Charlton from Leeds United, so he went instead to Tannadice and paid £30,000 for the man he knew would be the backbone of his first great side.

Shanks called Yeats 'a colossus in defence', and the description was an apt one. Within five months of his arrival in the summer of 1961 Yeats had been made skipper. In his first season the Reds galloped to promotion, not many centre-forwards finding a way past him. In the First Division Ron Yeats proved to be most dominant in the air, while on the ground his tremendous tackling and sensible distribution went to prove what a great asset he was. He was an inspiring captain, leading the club to two Championships and a succession of superb European matches.

The 1964/65 FA Cup campaign saw Yeats produce some of his most outstanding performances. In the third round at the Hawthorns he mistakenly picked up the ball in his own penalty area after somebody in the crowd blew a whistle. A penalty was awarded but justice was done when Albion's Bobby Cram blasted the ball high and wide. In the fifth round at Burnden Park Yeats pulled a muscle after only nine minutes but still went on to keep Wanderers' Welsh international centre-forward Wyn Davies in check. In the sixth round he laid on the winner for Roger Hunt and then completely dominated Leeds United and England centre-forward Alan Peacock.

Throughout the 1960s Yeats was still essentially a rugged centre-half but as the decade wore on he grew more accomplished. Off the field he was a great influence on the younger players in the Anfield team and, though quietly spoken, his imposing personality made him the ideal choice for dealing with the Liverpool management.

After losing his place to Larry Lloyd he still contributed a valuable spell at left-back. Nicknamed 'Rowdy' after Clint Eastwood's television cowboy of that era, he made the short trip to Prenton Park, becoming Tranmere Rovers' player-assistant manager and later manager. Yeats took many former Anfield men to

Prenton Park, including Bobby Graham, Ian St John, Willie Stevenson and Tommy Lawrence. Attendances began to soar as interest in the club was revitalised but in April 1975 he was sacked. He then had spells with Stalybridge Celtic and Barrow before he went into the haulage business and later the catering trade. A player who will go down in Liverpool folklore, Ron Yeats is now the Reds' chief scout.

ALEX YOUNG
Forward
Born 3.2.37, Loanhead

LEAGUE RECORD

	A	G
Everton	227 (1)	77
Stockport County	23	5

HONOURS
League Championship 1962/63
FA Cup 1965/66
8 Scotland Caps

ALEX YOUNG signed for Scottish club Heart of Midlothian from Newtongrange Star and made his debut as an eighteen-year-old. In five seasons with the Tynecastle club he scored seventy-seven goals, including twenty in the club's record-breaking 1957/58 Championship campaign and twenty-three when they recaptured the title in 1959/60. Young joined Everton in November 1960 in a £55,000 deal that also brought team-mate and full-back George Thomson to Goodison, and he soon won over the Blues' fans with his class. He didn't make his Everton debut until the following month because he arrived on Merseyside carrying a nasty knee injury sustained in playing for the British Army.

FACT

A television play centred around the Everton club in the 1960s was inspired by Alex Young. The play was entitled *The Golden Vision*.

In the Championship-winning season of 1962/63 Young scored in each of the opening three games, all victories. He ended the season with twenty-two goals, including the only goal of the game against Tottenham Hotspur that took Everton to the top of the League – a position from which they were never dislodged. He was arguably the greatest Scottish player to sign for Everton and was a major influence on the side that beat Sheffield Wednesday 3–2 in the 1966 FA Cup Final.

In attacking situations Young always seemed to have plenty of time. He knew where to play the ball instinctively – he didn't have to look where he was passing – and he was aware of all the options open to him without looking up. In addition to his flair and grace, he possessed a vicious shot and had good heading ability. Despite his subtlety, skill and natural ability, he only played for Scotland on eight occasions, making his debut in a 1–1 draw against England in 1960 – he surely should have played many more times. Like many players with flair and genius, he set himself very high standards and was often very critical of his own game. He was a gifted, elegant striker and when he was replaced near the end of his career there was a public outcry! He was replaced by a sixteen-year-old youngster by the name of Joe Royle for a game at Blackpool and manager Harry Catterick was assaulted by outraged Everton supporters – such was Young's popularity.

In August 1968 Young became player-manager of Glentoran. He only spent two months across the sea before returning to join Stockport County. Sadly, he was

forced to retire with knee trouble after just twenty-three games. He was one of the classiest players in post-war football and his fans worshipped him; to them he was simply the greatest!

On retirement, he returned north of the border and settled in Edinburgh, where he helps to run the family's wholesale business.

The Managers

SIR MATT BUSBY

One of the greatest names in the history of soccer and certainly the greatest name in the history of Manchester United, Matt Busby's playing days were actually spent with United's greatest rivals – Manchester City and Liverpool! He began his footballing days with Manchester City as a seventeen-year-old. At the time he was all set to emigrate to the United States with his mother but the City manager persuaded him to come to Maine Road instead. It was a decision that would change the course of his life. He played in 226 League and Cup games for City, starring in the 1933 and 1934 FA Cup Finals, picking up a winners' medal in the latter. He also won his one and only Scottish cap when he played against Wales in October 1933.

By the mid 1930s, City reckoned Busby's days were nearing their end and sold him to Liverpool. At Anfield, his flagging career was suddenly revived as he played alongside Tom Bradshaw and Jimmy McDougall in an all-Scottish half-back line. Though Busby remained on Liverpool's books until the end of the hostilities, the war spelled the end of his playing career. He was offered a job as Liverpool's assistant-manager but then out of the blue came a letter from Louis Rocca informing him that Manchester United were looking for a manager.

Set to become the longest-serving manager in United's history, Busby took the club to runners-up in the League on four occasions in the next five years before they finally carried off the title in 1951/52. They also won the FA Cup in 1948. It was Busby's first great team. A few years later came his second outstanding side, the famous Busby Babes who won two League Championships before being so cruelly destroyed at Munich. Busby himself was severely injured in the disaster but pulled through and made it to Wembley, only to see his brave team lose to Bolton Wanderers.

Busby was determined to build another great side and the reconstruction work began immediately. By the mid-1960s, he had put together a team that could rival his previous Championship sides. And with Best, Charlton and Law in the line-up they won the European Cup in 1968. A year later Busby decided to retire and Wilf McGuinness took over. It didn't work out and in December 1970 Busby stepped in again, finally quitting the manager's chair in the summer of 1971. He was promptly made a director of the club. He was awarded the CBE, knighted after winning the European Cup and made a Freeman of Manchester in 1967, subsequently becoming the club's president.

HARRY CATTERICK

Harry Catterick transformed Everton into a great footballing side, capable of living with the best. He was appointed manager in 1961 and was given a simple brief by John Moores: to get Everton Football Club back to the top by means of good, entertaining football. Catterick proved very adept at wheeling and dealing in the transfer market and brought some top-class players to Goodison Park, including Tony Kay, Johnny Morrissey, Fred Pickering, Gordon West and Ray Wilson. In his first season in charge he guided the Blues to fourth place in the First Division and twelve months later the revival he had sparked off reached its climax as the Blues won their sixth League Championship title in style. In 1966 Everton reached the FA Cup Final at Wembley and Catterick's biggest gamble – the inclusion of Cornishman Mike Trebilcock – paid off; he scored twice in a 3–2 win over Sheffield Wednesday.

As his youth policy began to pay off with John Hurst, Jimmy Husband and Joe Royle all fighting their way into the first team, Catterick signed Alan Ball and a new Everton side began to take shape. In 1968 he took the club back to Wembley, only for their opponents West Bromwich Albion to snatch the FA Cup in extra time. By the start of the 1969/70 season Harry Catterick had built one of the finest club sides of post-war English football. The Blues swept to the League title as Ball, Harvey and Kendall controlled the midfield but within a year the club had slumped to fourteenth place with the Everton manager unable to explain why his side had run out of confidence.

In January 1972, while driving home from Sheffield, he had a heart attack. In April 1973, with four years of his contract still to run, the club moved him sideways into a senior executive role. Sadly, the man who restored so much pride to Everton died at Goodison Park after an FA Cup quarter-final match against Ipswich Town in March 1985.

TOMMY DOCHERTY

The irrepressible Tommy Docherty was one of the best-known managers in soccer. He began his playing career with Glasgow Celtic but soon moved to Preston North End where he developed into a fine wing-half. He helped the Lilywhites win the Second Division Championship in 1950/51 and had played in over 350 League and Cup games when he moved to Arsenal in August 1958 after Preston had refused him permission to play in that summer's World Cup Finals!

Stamford Bridge was his next port of call when he signed as player-coach in February 1961. When manager Ted Drake left the following September, Docherty became caretaker-manager and was given the job permanently in January 1962. He could not prevent Chelsea's relegation that season, but they bounced straight back again the following term. The League Cup was won in 1965 and the Doc also took Chelsea to their first Wembley FA Cup Final where they lost 2–1 to Spurs.

Docherty broke Chelsea's transfer record four times, with signings such as Graham Moore, Charlie Cooke and Tony Hateley. He also sold many of the Blues' favourites, including Terry Venables and George Graham. Life was never boring when the Doc was around. He once sent home eight Chelsea first-teamers from their training headquarters at Blackpool as a punishment for staying out too late at night. He even rebelled against the Chelsea directors over the players' allocation of tickets for an FA Cup tie and threatened to call off a tour to Bermuda – for which he later received a 28-day suspension!

In October 1967 he resigned as Chelsea manager and took over the reins at Rotherham United. After failing to prevent the Millers' relegation, he was lured to Queen's Park Rangers but sensationally quit after only twenty-nine days in charge. His next appointment was as manager of Aston Villa, who were struggling in the Second Division. Though they avoided relegation, the following season was one of the worst in the club's history and in January 1970 Docherty was sacked. He then managed Porto of Portugal, his side just missing the Portuguese Championship by two points.

Docherty returned to become Scotland's national team manager and restored the team's pride. Then in December 1972 he accepted an offer to manage Manchester United, helping them win the FA Cup in 1977. After a short spell with Derby County he took charge of Queen's Park Rangers again. His next move was to Australia to manage Sydney Olympic but in June 1981 he returned to manage his former club, Preston North End. Docherty's last managerial post in the Football League was with Wolverhampton Wanderers, but since then he has been an after-dinner speaker.

RON GREENWOOD

The West Ham United manager gained a reputation for his tactical genius and knowledge of the game. His sides played with attacking flair and even if they weren't as successful as they could have been they were always a delight to watch.

Greenwood made his debut in senior football as a wartime guest for Chelsea but as he wasn't assured of first-team football there he joined Bradford Park Avenue. Three seasons later he moved back to London to play for Brentford where he enjoyed his best playing days. A stylish centre-half, he returned to Stamford Bridge in 1952, helping Chelsea win the League Championship in 1954/55. He later ended his playing days with Fulham, where he qualified as a coach. He coached Walthamstow Avenue before taking up his first managerial post with Eastbourne United in 1957. As a close friend of England manager Walter Winterbottom, he was invited to run England's Youth and Under-23 sides of the late 1950s.

In November 1958 he became Arsenal's assistant-manager and stayed at Highbury until 1961 when he was appointed manager of West Ham United. Only the fourth such appointment in the club's history, he was the first West Ham manager to have no previous connection with the club. The Hammers won the FA Cup in 1964 and a year later were back at Wembley, this time to lift the European Cup Winners' Cup. Greenwood developed England's World Cup winning trio of Bobby Moore, Geoff Hurst and Martin Peters and also brought a number of expensive players to the club, including Peter Brabrook, Johnny Byrne and Billy Bonds. After reaching the League Cup Final of 1966, the Hammers suffered some lean years and Greenwood didn't endear himself to the West Ham faithful when he allowed Martin Peters to join Spurs, with Jimmy Greaves moving in the opposite direction – he cared little for players' reputations. In 1971, after the Hammers had lost 4–0 to Blackpool in an FA Cup tie, it was reported that Bobby Moore and three other players had been seen at a nightclub the evening before the game. Greenwood imposed a heavy fine on them and withdrew Moore's captaincy.

At the end of the 1973/74 season Greenwood became the club's general manager and John Lyall took over as team manager. In December 1977 he was selected to take over from Don Revie as the England manager. He guided England to the Finals of the 1980 European Championship and the 1982 World Cup Finals before retiring after five years in charge of the national team.

JOE MERCER

One of the game's all-time greats, Joe Mercer enjoyed a great career as a player and a manager. He began his career as a junior with Everton in 1932 and stayed with them until 1946. In that time he developed into one of the finest wing-halves in the country and helped the Toffees to the League Championship in 1938/39. When war came he lost seven seasons of top-class soccer but played regularly in wartime, being part of a famous England half-back line with Stan Cullis and Cliff Britton. Out of favour with Everton, he moved to Arsenal where his career was rejuvenated.

He led the Gunners first clear of relegation, then to the League Championship in 1947/48 as captain. He played in his first FA Cup Final for the club in 1950 when they beat Liverpool; two seasons later they lost to Newcastle United in the final. Mercer was voted 'Footballer of the Year' in 1950 and gained another League Championship medal in 1952/53. His illustrious career came to an end when he broke his leg in April 1954 against Blackpool at Highbury, just before his fortieth birthday.

Mercer went into management, first with Sheffield United and then Aston Villa. At Villa Park he saw the club promoted from the Second Division, reach two FA Cup semi-finals and win the League Cup. However, in 1964 Mercer suffered a stroke as a result of over-work. The Villa directors waited until he was over the worst effects, then sacked him. Most people thought his enforced retirement would be permanent but in July 1965 he made a comeback as manager of Manchester City. Along with his assistant Malcolm Allison, Mercer revitalised a club that had been in the doldrums for far too long. City won the Second Division title in 1965/66, then the League Championship two years later. More trophies followed as City beat Leicester in the 1969 FA Cup Final and then took the European Cup Winners' Cup the following year.

In June 1972 Mercer moved to become general manager of Coventry City and in 1974 took temporary charge of the England team. He was awarded an OBE for his services to football in 1976. In 1981 he resigned from the Coventry board after six years as a director at Highfield Road. Subsequently he lived in retirement on Merseyside until his death in August 1990.

BILL NICHOLSON

One of the greatest managers of British soccer, Bill Nicholson was the architect of one of the finest club sides the world has ever seen. In the early 1960s his Spurs team played exhilarating, flowing football. They won the League and FA Cup 'double' in 1960/61, the first club to do so in the twentieth century. This remarkable triumph was followed by a steady stream of Cup successes as Spurs went marching on.

Nicholson joined the club as a groundstaff boy in March 1936 and was farmed out to Spurs' nursery club, Northfleet, where he developed over the next two years. In 1938 he signed professional forms and made his debut at left-back at Blackburn some two months later. His career was soon interrupted by the war and when he returned to White Hart Lane after the hostilities he turned out at centre-half before establishing himself at right-half. He played in Arthur Rowe's side which won the Second Division Championship in 1949/50 and the League title the season after. His one and only appearance for England, against Portugal at Goodison Park, saw him score from long range with his first kick of the game after a matter of seconds. He made 345 League and Cup appearances for Spurs before retiring in 1954 to take up a coaching post within the club. In August 1957 he became assistant-manager and then in October 1958 took over from Jimmy Anderson as manager.

His first game in charge saw Spurs beat Everton 10–4! He began to develop sides with great style and allowed his players to show off their skills and entertain the crowds. Success came on the field and Spurs' 'double'-winning side of 1960/61 was one of the greatest-ever club line-ups in English soccer. The following season they won the FA Cup again and in 1963 they won their first European trophy when they beat Athletico Madrid 5–1 in the European Cup Winners' Cup Final. He was in the process of rebuilding the Spurs side when they won the FA Cup again in 1967. They also won the League Cup in 1971 and 1973 and the UEFA Cup in 1972.

After a poor start to the 1974/75 season Nicholson surprised most people by resigning as manager after sixteen years in charge. The players and directors tried to persuade him to change his mind but to no avail. He took a deserved rest from the game before returning to work as consultant to West Ham United but within months he was back at White Hart Lane as chief adviser and scout. He was awarded the OBE in 1975, a testimonial game at Spurs in August 1983 and the PFA Merit Award in 1984. In May 1991 Bill Nicholson was appointed Spurs' president, a position he still holds.

HARRY POTTS

Burnley's most successful manager, Harry Potts was one of the first products of the club's youth policy. He joined the Turf Moor club in November 1937 but war broke out just as he looked likely to make a big impact in the game. He spent a large part of the war with the RAF in the Far East and in 1945 was a member of Denis Compton's star-studded team which toured India. He also 'guested' for Sunderland and Fulham during the Second World War.

He made his Football League debut for Burnley in the opening game of the 1946/47 season, ending the campaign as the club's leading scorer with fifteen goals in forty games as the Clarets won promotion to the First Division. The club also reached the FA Cup Final, only to lose 1–0 to Charlton Athletic. Potts continued to top the club's scoring charts for the next three seasons but in October 1950, after scoring fifty goals in 181 games, he left to play for Everton before being appointed chief coach at Wolverhampton Wanderers in the summer of 1956. A year later he took over as manager of Shrewsbury Town before taking charge of Burnley in January 1958.

After inheriting the nucleus of a fine side, he led the Clarets to the League Championship in 1959/60. In the FA Cup Final in 1962, they lost 3–1 to Spurs. They entered European football for the first time and gave a good account of themselves in the European Cup. They also reached the semi-final of the League Cup but lost to Aston Villa in the third game.

When Potts sold Jimmy McIlroy to Stoke City for £25,000, many fans were so angry that they refused to attend Turf Moor for the club's home games. With attendances dwindling, Potts was forced to sell Burnley's star players and over the years the heart was ripped out of the club by the sale of John Connelly, Alex Elder, Willie Irvine, Andy Lochhead and Willie Morgan.

In February 1970 Potts became the club's general manager, ending twelve years of the most successful period in Burnley's history. He left Turf Moor in July 1972 but the following year took over the reins at Blackpool. Though the Seasiders were always challenging for a place in the top flight, they never made it and in May 1976 Potts lost his job. Two months later he returned to Turf Moor as chief scout before again being appointed Burnley manager in February 1977. In 1978/79 the club won the Anglo-Scottish Cup but after a poor start to the 1979/80 season Potts was sacked. He later scouted for the now defunct Colne Dynamoes.

SIR ALF RAMSEY

As a player, Alf Ramsey was a strong, polished and distinguished defender, who joined Portsmouth as an amateur in 1942 and a year later moved to The Dell to play for Southampton. He made his England debut in a 6–0 victory over Switzerland at Highbury in December 1948 before going on to make twenty-eight consecutive appearances for his country. In all he won thirty-two caps for England and represented the Football League on five occasions. In May 1949 he moved to Tottenham Hotspur for £21,000, a record fee for a full-back. Virtually ever-present in the teams that won the Second Division and Football League titles in 1949/50 and 1950/51, he was very accurate with penalties and free-kicks and developed into a great reader of the game.

In May 1955, after appearing in 250 League and Cup games for the White Hart Lane club, Ramsay retired. He was appointed manager of Ipswich Town in August 1955 and immediately began to refashion the Portman Road side in a manner which was to herald the dawn of a new era. He led the club to the Third Division (South) title in 1956/57, the Second Division Championship in 1960/61 and the First Division Championship in 1961/62.

In January 1963 he was appointed the full-time manager of England. His greatest triumph came in 1966 when England, playing on home territory, won the World Cup for the first and only time. In May 1974, after England had failed to qualify for the finals of that year's World Cup competition, he was sacked. Under Alf Ramsey, England played 113 games. They won sixty-nine of them and lost only seventeen. In September 1977, at the age of fifty-seven, Sir Alf was appointed manager of Birmingham City. He held office for only six months before being forced to relinquish the position owing to ill-health. His final appointment in 1980 saw him take the post of technical director with Panathinaikos but his stay with the Athenian club lasted only a few months.

DON REVIE

Don Revie was one of the great managers of his era, transforming Leeds United from a struggling Second Division side into one of the most powerful and successful teams in Europe.

Revie joined Leicester City towards the end of the Second World War and helped them reach the FA Cup Final with two goals in the semi-final victory over Portsmouth. He then had a spell with Hull City but, following the departure of player-manager Raich Carter, he left to join Manchester City. At Maine Road Revie hit the headlines as the tactical architect of the 'Revie Plan'. By 1954/55 City were one of the top sides in the First Division. Revie was capped by England and in 1955 was voted 'Footballer of the Year'. Revie appeared for Manchester City in the 1955 FA Cup Final, which they lost 3–1 to Newcastle United. However, the following year they beat Birmingham City 3–1 in the final – Revie only played because first-choice Billy Spurdle was injured. In November 1956 Revie was on the move again, this time to Sunderland, but within two years he had joined Leeds United, where he was later to make a name for himself as one of the most successful managers of all time.

Revie's managerial career got off to a slow start as Leeds narrowly avoided relegation in 1961/62. However, the development of a youth policy enabled Revie to produce players like Gary Sprake, Paul Reaney and Norman Hunter. The club won the Second Division Championship in 1963/64 and then made an immediate impact on the top flight as Revie bought wisely on the transfer market. In the First Division Leeds came close to the Championship on a number of occasions. They were League Champions in 1968/69 and 1973/74 and were runners-up no fewer than four times during Revie's period of control. The 1968/69 season was a record-breaking one with sixty-seven points gained and only two defeats recorded during the entire season. Leeds reached four FA Cup Finals, winning only one in 1972. They also won the League Cup in 1968 and had an excellent record in European competitions. They won the Inter Cities Fairs Cup in 1968 and 1971 and reached the European Cup Winners' Cup Final in 1973.

In July 1974 Revie was appointed manager of England but was a complete disaster in the role. He negotiated a massively paid coaching job in the United Arab Emirates. He was bitterly criticised by both the FA and the Press and was later suspended from British soccer until he was willing to face a charge of bringing the game into disrepute. He was later banned for ten years from English soccer but eventually won a High Court case against the FA and was guaranteed an injunction quashing the ban.

In the late 1980s he was struck down by motor neurone disease and in his last years was confined to a wheelchair.

BILL SHANKLY

The most legendary figure in the history of Liverpool Football Club, Bill Shankly turned the Second Division side into one of the most famous clubs in world soccer. He began his career with Carlisle United but after just sixteen appearances joined Preston North End. He went on to play in over three hundred games for the Deepdale club, though the war robbed him of many more games.

In March 1949 Shankly was offered his first chance in management at his former club Carlisle. He remained there just two years before Grimsby Town tempted him with another managerial post. That job lasted almost four years before he surprisingly quit to join struggling Workington Town. A year later he was on the move again, this time as assistant to Andy Beattie at Huddersfield

Town. Within a year Town had been relegated and Beattie sacked. Shankly was immediately appointed manager, a post which lasted for three years before Liverpool, then in the Second Division, stepped in with an offer.

Most of the players he inherited at Anfield were transferred, new players were bought and even the club's training ground at Melwood was refurbished. Shankly's first success came in 1961/62 as Liverpool lifted the Second Division Championship. Two years later they were League Champions and followed that up in 1965 by winning the FA Cup for the first time in their history. Over the next nine years, as Bill Shankly ruled supreme, Liverpool lifted two more League titles as well as the FA Cup for a second time and the UEFA Cup.

In 1974, following Liverpool's FA Cup victory, Bill Shankly shocked the football world by resigning. There had been no hint of it, although he had often threatened to resign over matters of principle in the past. However, it wasn't long before he missed the game and he was soon taking on consultancy roles. Sadly, he was never offered any other post at Anfield, not even a directorship, and in his later years he felt very bitter about the way the club had treated him.

Bill Shankly died on 29 September 1981, a few days after suffering a heart attack. He was, without doubt, one of the greatest managers of the modern era, turning a sleeping giant into the great club it is today.

Statistics

Best XI

Selecting a 'best' team can be fascinating but it can also be highly provocative. Below is my best team selected from the hundred players included in this book.

1. Gordon Banks
2. George Cohen
3. Ray Wilson
4. Danny Blanchflower
5. Jack Charlton
6. Bobby Moore
7. George Best
8. Denis Law
9. Bobby Charlton
10. Johnny Giles
11. Jimmy McIlroy
12. Jimmy Greaves

Top Tens

MOST LEAGUE APPEARANCES

1.	Terry Paine	824
2.	Alan Oakes	776
3.	Billy Bonds	758
4.	Pat Jennings	757
5.=	Alan Ball	743
	John Hollins	743
7.	Ian Callaghan	731
8.	Martin Peters	722
9=	Ron Harris	716
	Mike Summerbee	716

MOST GOALS

1.	Jimmy Greaves	357
2.	Ron Davies	275
3.	Roger Hunt	269
4.	Kevin Hector	268
5.	Bryan 'Pop' Robson	265
6.	Francis Lee	228
7.	Allan Clarke	223
8.	Derek Dougan	222
9.	Bobby Smith	218
10.	Denis Law	217

MOST LEAGUE APPEARANCES (ONE CLUB)

1.	Terry Paine (Southampton)	713
2.	Billy Bonds (West Ham United)	663
3.	Ron Harris (Chelsea)	655
4.	Jack Charlton (Leeds United)	628
5.	Bobby Charlton (Manchester United)	606
6.	Peter Bonetti (Chelsea)	600
7.	Johnny Haynes (Fulham)	594
8.	Ronnie Clayton (Blackburn Rovers)	581
9.	Jimmy Armfield (Blackpool)	568
10.	Alan Oakes (Manchester City)	564

MOST GOALS (ONE CLUB)

1.	Roger Hunt (Liverpool)	245
2.	Jimmy Greaves (Tottenham Hotspur)	220
3.	Bobby Charlton (Manchester United)	199
4.	Geoff Hurst (West Ham United)	180
5.	Denis Law (Manchester United)	171
6.	Peter Lorimer (Leeds United)	168
7.	Bobby Tambling (Chelsea)	164
8.	Terry Paine (Southampton)	160
9.	Kevin Hector (Derby County)	155
10.	Don Rogers (Swindon Town)	148

MOST INTERNATIONAL APPEARANCES

1.	Pat Jennings (Northern Ireland)	119
2.	Bobby Moore (England)	108
3.	Bobby Charlton (England)	106
4.	Gordon Banks (England)	73
5.	Alan Ball (England)	72
6.	Martin Peters (England)	67
7.	Ray Wilson (England)	63
8.=	Johnny Giles (Republic of Ireland)	59
	Cliff Jones (Wales)	59
10.	Jimmy Greaves (England)	57